AF600735

The Best of
Frank Kunert

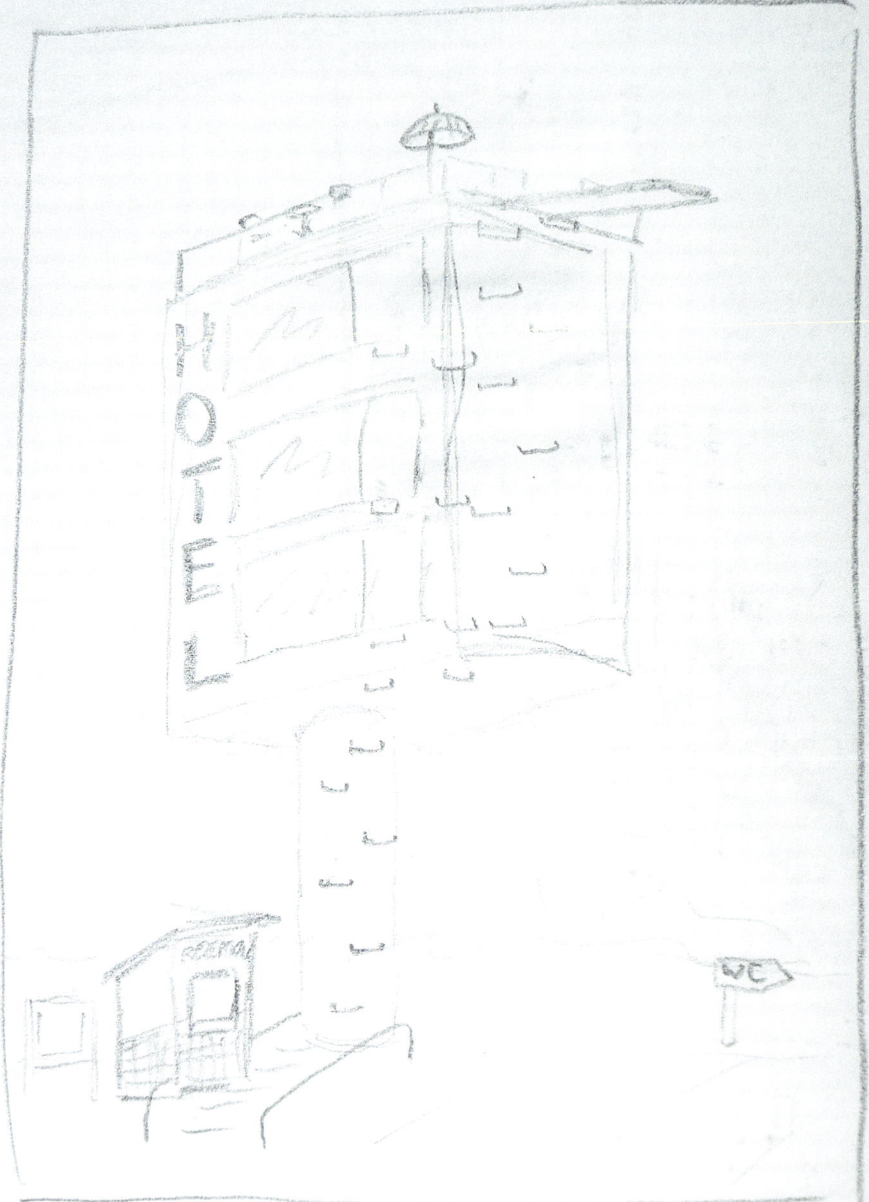

„Kletterhaus“ 11.6.17

The Best of
Frank Kunert

Mit einem Text von
With a text by
Ariadne von Schirach

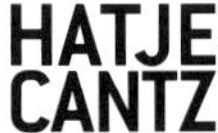

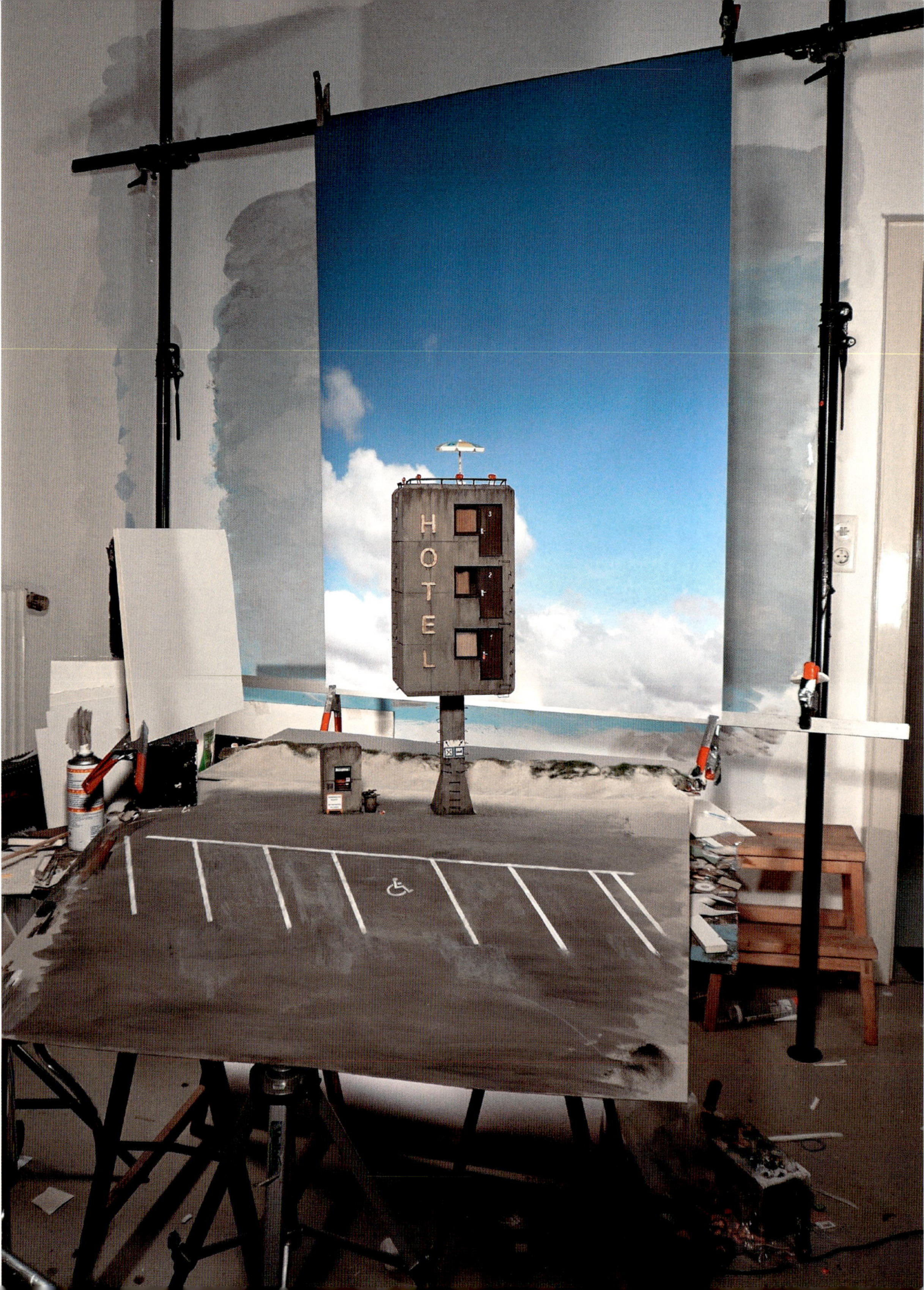
HOTEL

Ich bin dann mal träumen

Ariadne von Schirach

Beim ersten Blick auf Frank Kunerts Bilder empfand ich Freude und ein Gefühl von Trost. Die Welt brennt, Kriege, Krisen, Klimawandel, da ist es nicht leicht, an den Menschen zu glauben. Oder an seine Habitate. Doch dieser Fotograf schien allem eine gewisse Bewohnbarkeit abzutrotzen, kleine Orte, an denen das Leben präzise, geordnet und vergnüglich wirkte. Was für ein gutes Auge, dachte ich, und fragte mich, wohin er für seine Bilder wohl reise.

Der zweite Blick offenbarte Verstörenderes. Verschobene Fenster, seltsame Rampen himmelwärts, unpraktische Tische. Mir kamen immer unabweisbarere Zweifel an meiner Einschätzung, bis ich begriff, dass hier jemand nicht *unsere* Wirklichkeit fotografierte, sondern seine eigene. Diese inneren Bilder werden zu Skizzen, welche der Künstler mit größter Präzision im Miniaturformat erbaut und dann in seinem Studio arrangiert, ausleuchtet und festhält. Kunert ist also durchaus ein Reisender, doch er reist nicht ans andere Ende der Welt, sondern in den Weltinnenraum, wie Rilke es nennt, in unser ebenso individuelles wie kollektives Unterbewusstsein, wo sich Bewusstes und Unbewusstes, Schönes und Absurdes, Fantasien und Wahrheit vermischen.

Und so skurril und einzigartig jedes einzelne Werk Kunerts ist, so zeigen sich auch in dieser ersten Überblicksschau gewisse Muster. Wiederkehrende Themen wie Alter, Vergänglichkeit und Tod, gelingende und unmögliche Kommunikation, große Erwartungen und das alltägliche Scheitern, stets getragen von einem ansteckenden Sinn für das Absurde, von dem Camus einst sagte, es sei die erhellte Vernunft, die ihre Grenzen feststelle.

Diese Aporien des Alltags zeigen sich auch in wiederkehrenden Elementen wie Toiletten oder Sprungbrettern, welche den Raum des Gewohnten öffnen, um dahinterliegende emotionale Wahrheiten sichtbar zu machen. Für Kunert markieren die Sprungbretter Schwebezustände, sind Orte von Gefahr und Neubeginn. Die Toiletten symbolisieren unter anderem den Umstand, dass in unserer Mediengesellschaft eine Neigung dazu besteht, auch kleine, unappetitliche Abgründe in die Öffentlichkeit loszulassen, das Unzerkaute, den »Abhub«, wie Walter Benjamin es nannte.

Vielleicht steckt in dieser Kritik, die so alt ist wie die Massenmedien, auch eine Antwort auf die Frage, was Kunst heute noch ist und sein kann. Denn obwohl Kunert sich in seinen Werken bewusst auf eigene Erfahrungen bezieht – vieles sieht aus wie aus den Sechzigern, seiner Kindheit, die imaginäre Architektur ist zumeist deutsch, und auch für emotionale Lagen, die sich in den Szenerien entbergen, schöpft der Künstler aus seinem eigenen Erleben –, verwandelt und veredelt er diese Affekte und Perzepte für uns alle.

Kunst macht Unsichtbares sichtbar. Dafür geht sie den Weg vom Besonderen des eigenen Erlebens zu etwas Allgemeinem, in dem sich die Betrachtenden wiedererkennen können, wenn sie wollen. In diesem Übersetzen, Gestalten, Transformieren liegen Nutzen und Würde künstlerischer Arbeit, welche beharrlich den eigenen Mist in feines Gold verwandelt. Auch über Kunerts Werken liegt ein Magritte-hafter Zauber, eine heitere Schönheit, die unaufdringlich mit den in den Tiefen der Bilder aufscheinenden Widersprüchen wie dem Abgrund zwischen Wunsch und Wirklichkeit oder einem Gewahrwerden der Einsamkeit, welche uns ebenso trennt wie verbindet, versöhnt. Denn die Menschen, die seine menschenleeren Szenerien bewohnen, stehen *vor* den Bildern und sind eingeladen, sich selbst in Ratlosigkeit und Staunen zu erkennen, in Vergänglichkeit, Humor und den Beziehungen zu allem, was um uns ist.

Die Welt ist immer schon vorhanden, und die Kunst erinnert uns daran, dass wir sie gestalten können. Doch zugleich müssen wir sie auch bewohnen und bewahren. In dieser auch in Kunerts Werken so deutlichen Anerkennung des Gewesenen und Mit-uns-Seienden liegt gerade in Zeiten der Krise eine kühle Absage an hitzige Weltrettungsfantasien. Dazu schreibt Donna Haraway in ihrem Buch *Unruhig bleiben*: »Ich fühle mich zutiefst den bescheideneren Möglichkeiten der teilweisen Erholung und dem gemeinsamen Weitermachen verpflichtet.«

Dieses gemeinsame Weitermachen, genau da, wo man ist, mit dem, was um einen ist, befähigt uns, das Geheimnis des Lebens immer wieder neu in eine Heimat zu verwandeln. Und das ist ebenso ein Aufbruch wie eine Heimkehr – zu uns selbst und zur Natur ebenso wie zu unseren eigenen Schöpfungen.

Auch aus Kunerts Bildern spricht ein tiefes Gefühl für die Würde der Dinge, Objekte und Gebäude. Letztere schneidet er aus Leichtschaumplatten und lässt dann geduldig an den bemalten Fassaden die Zeit vergehen; eine Schramme hier, ein Schatten dort. Dabei entstehen Nester aus Beton, flauschige Festungen im Stil eines postapokalyptischen und dennoch zärtlichen Brutalismus, surreal und bewohnbar zugleich.

Und so lässt uns der Künstler nicht nur einen selbstironischen Blick auf unsere eigene menschliche Verfasstheit werfen, sondern auch auf das geheime Leben unserer Bauten. Und manchmal, so will mir beim Betrachten scheinen, blicken diese gar zurück.

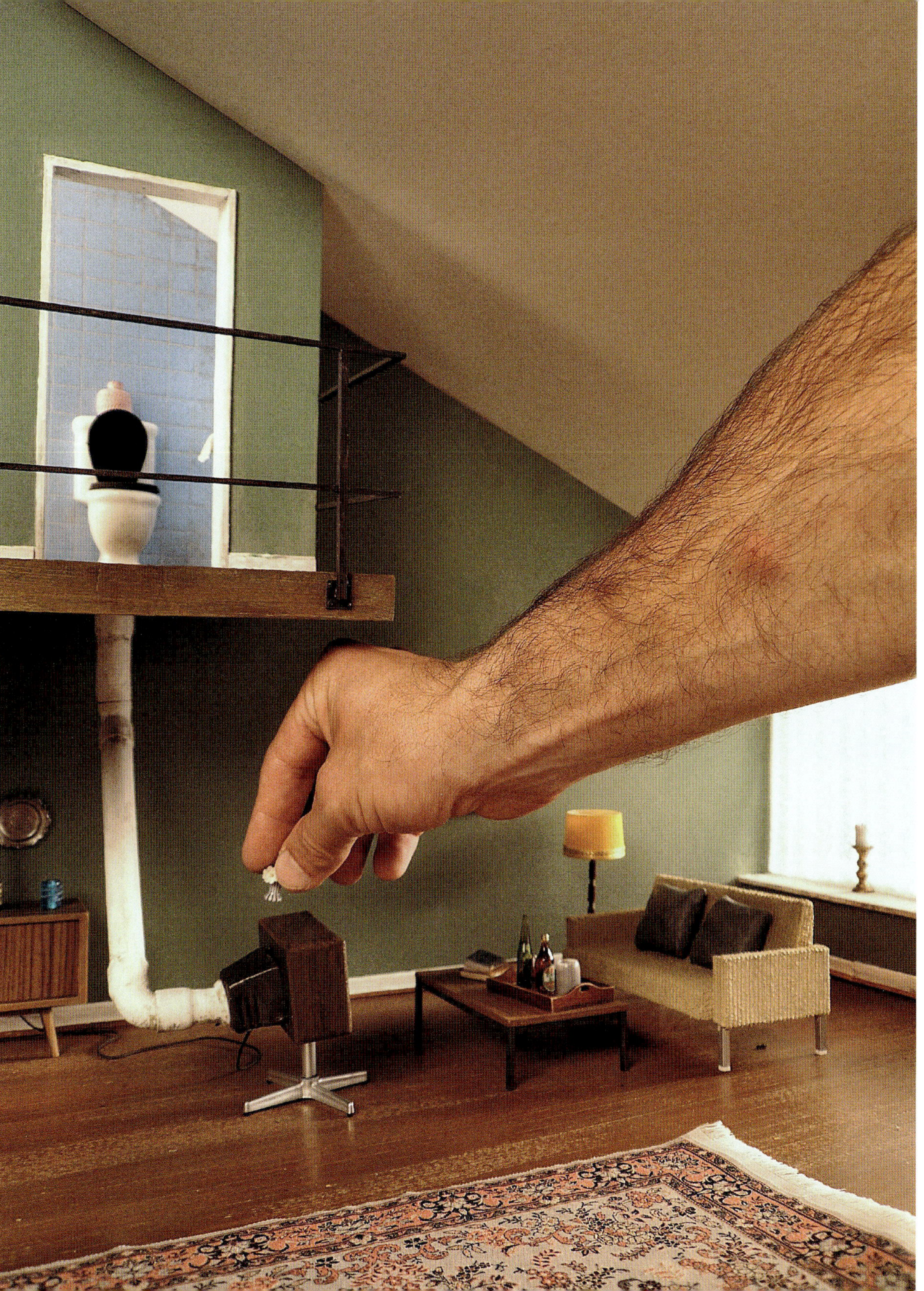

I'm Off to Dream

Ariadne von Schirach

When I first looked at Frank Kunert's photographs, I felt joy and a sense of consolation. The world is burning – wars, crises, climate change – so it is not easy to still believe in people. Or in their habitats. Yet this photographer seemed to wrest a certain habitability from everything: small places where life appeared to be precise, ordered, and pleasant. What a good eye, I thought, and asked myself where he traveled for his photographs.

A second look revealed something more disturbing. Displaced windows, strange ramps leading skyward, impractical tables. I started to have even more undeniable doubts about my assessment until I realized that this was not someone photographing *our* reality but rather his own. These inner images become sketches which the artist with great precision transforms into miniature scenes and then arranges, illuminates, and captures in his studio. Kunert is thus by all means a traveler, yet he travels not to the other end of the world but rather into the world interior, as Rilke calls it, into our equally individual and collective subconscious, where the conscious and the unconscious, the beautiful and the absurd, fantasies and truth intertwine. Although every single one of Kunert's works is a world of its own, this first overview does also reveal certain patterns. Recurring themes such as age, transience, and death, successful and impossible communication, great expectations and everyday failure, always borne by an infectious sense of the absurd, of which Camus once said that it is "lucid reason noting its limits."

These quotidian aporias are deepened by recurring elements such as toilets or diving boards that open the space of the familiar to unveil the emotional truths behind it. For Kunert, the diving boards mark states of suspense, are places of danger and new beginning. The toilets symbolize, among other things, the penchant of our media society for releasing to the public even small, unappetizing abysses, the unchewed, the *Abhub* or waste, as Walter Benjamin called it.

Maybe this criticism, which is as old as mass media, also holds an answer to the question of what art still is and can be today. For although Kunert intentionally refers to his own experiences in his works – much of it looks like something from the 1960s, the era of his childhood, the imaginary architecture is mainly German, and the artist also draws on his own lived experience for the emotional states disclosed in his scenarios – he transforms and ennobles these affects and percepts for all of us.

Art makes the invisible visible. To do so, it takes the path from the uniqueness of one's own experience to something universal within that experience in which viewers can recognize themselves if they wish. The benefits and dignity of artistic work lie in the translation, creation, and transformation, which persistently turns one's own muck into fine gold. A Magritte-like enchantment also gilds Kunert's works, a cheerful beauty that unobtrusively reconciles the viewers with the contradictions that appear in his work's depths like the abyss between wish and reality or an awareness of the loneliness that both separates and connects us all. Indeed, the people who inhabit Kunert's deserted scenes stand *in front of* the pictures and are invited to recognize themselves in perplexity and amazement, in frailty, humor, and our many relationships to everything that is around us.

The world is always present, and art reminds us that we can shape it. At the same time, however, we also have to inhabit and preserve it. In this recognition both of the past and of everything that is with us, which is very prominent in Kunert's works, lies, especially in times of crisis, a cool rejection of heated world-saving fantasies. Donna Haraway explicates this mature and humble perspective in her book *Staying with the Trouble*: "I am deeply committed to the more modest possibilities of partial recuperation and getting on together."

These possibilities of world-making and getting on together – precisely where we are, with what surrounds us – enable us to transform the secret of life into temporary yet inhabitable dwellings, again and again. And this is as much a departure as it is a returning home – to ourselves, to nature, and to our own creations.

Kunert's works express a profound appreciation for the dignity of things, objects, and buildings. The latter he carves from lightweight foam boards and then patiently lets time pass on their painted façades; a scratch here, a shadow there. This results in lairs of concrete, fleecy fortresses in the style of a postapocalyptic and yet tender Brutalism – surreal and homey at the same time.

And so the artist has cast a self-ironic eye not only onto our own human condition but also onto the secret life of our buildings. And when I take a very close look, sometimes it seems to me that they are even gazing back.

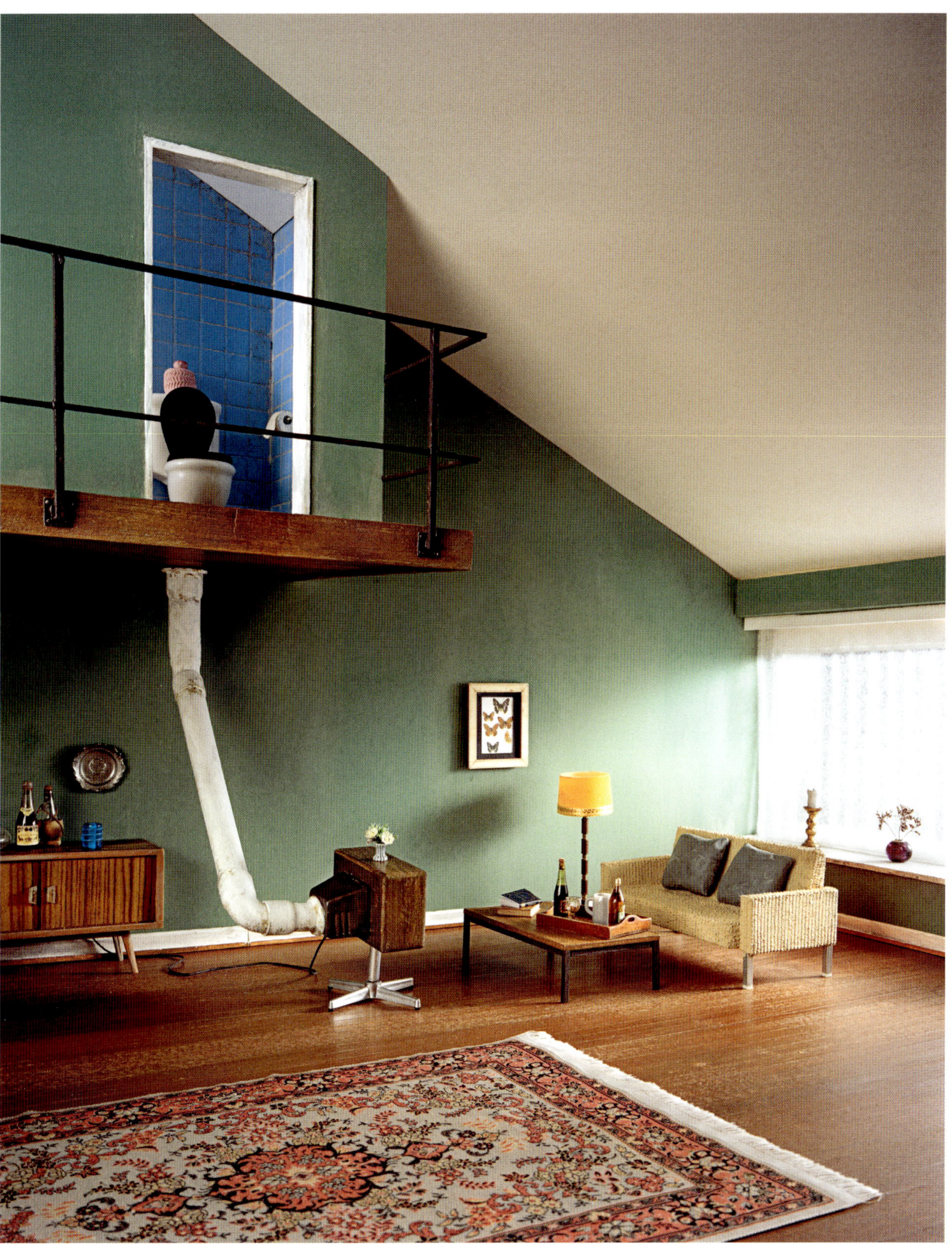

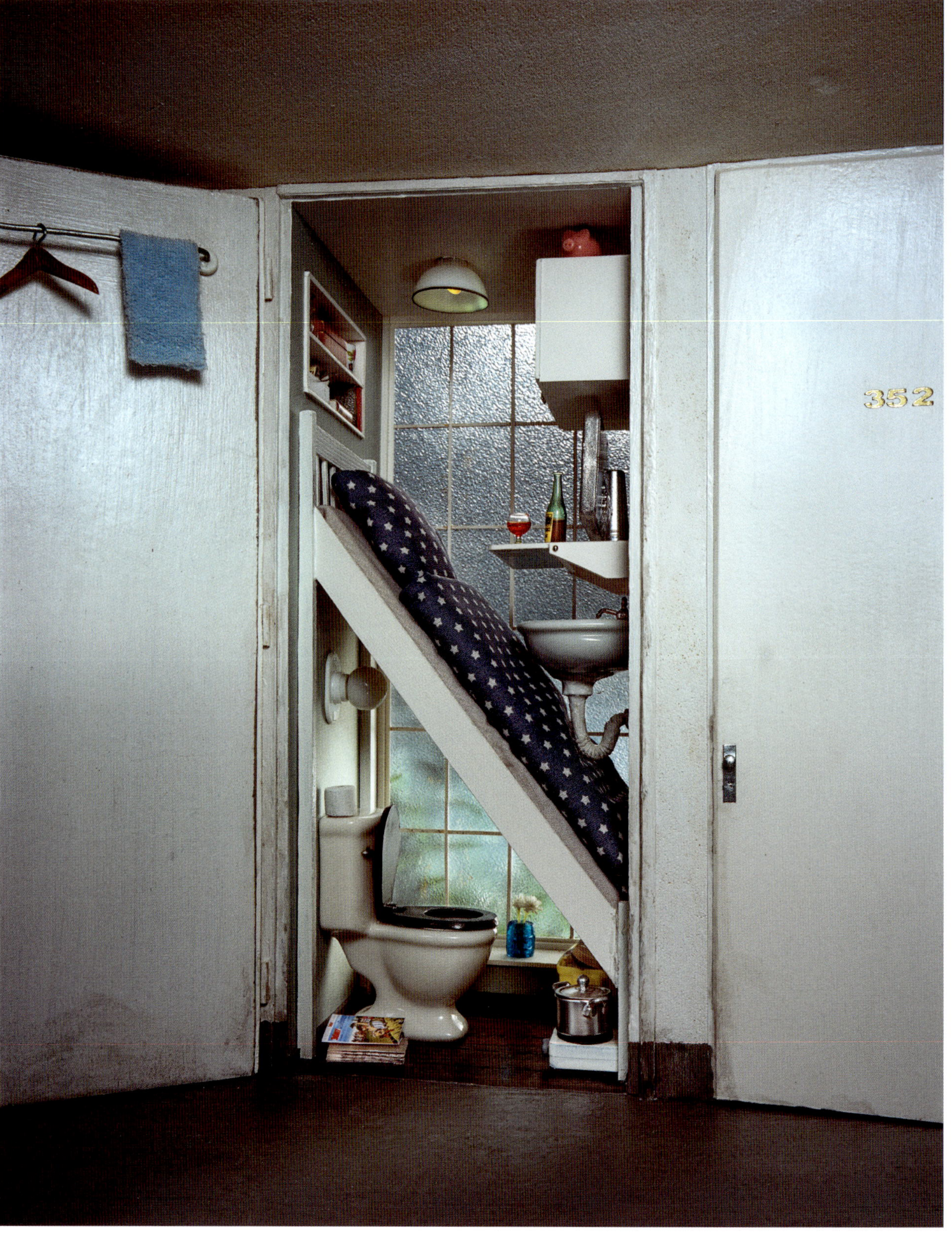
352

Ein-Zimmer-Apartment |
One Bedroom Apartment
2016

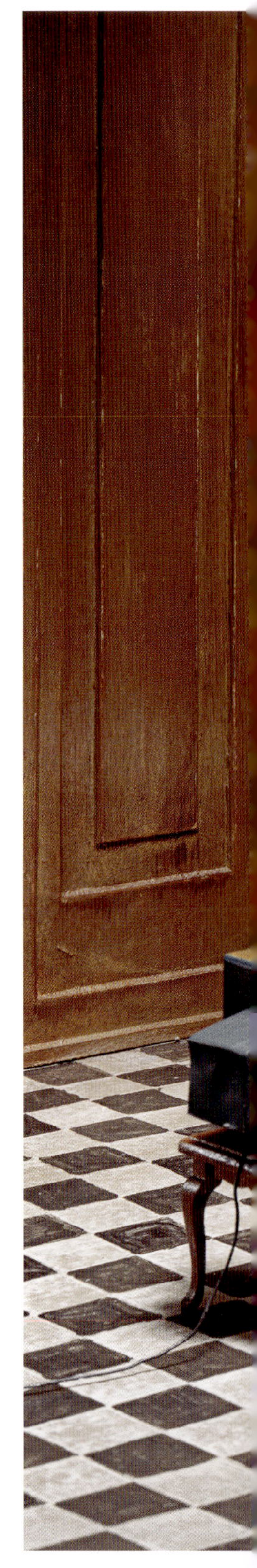

Menu à deux
2009

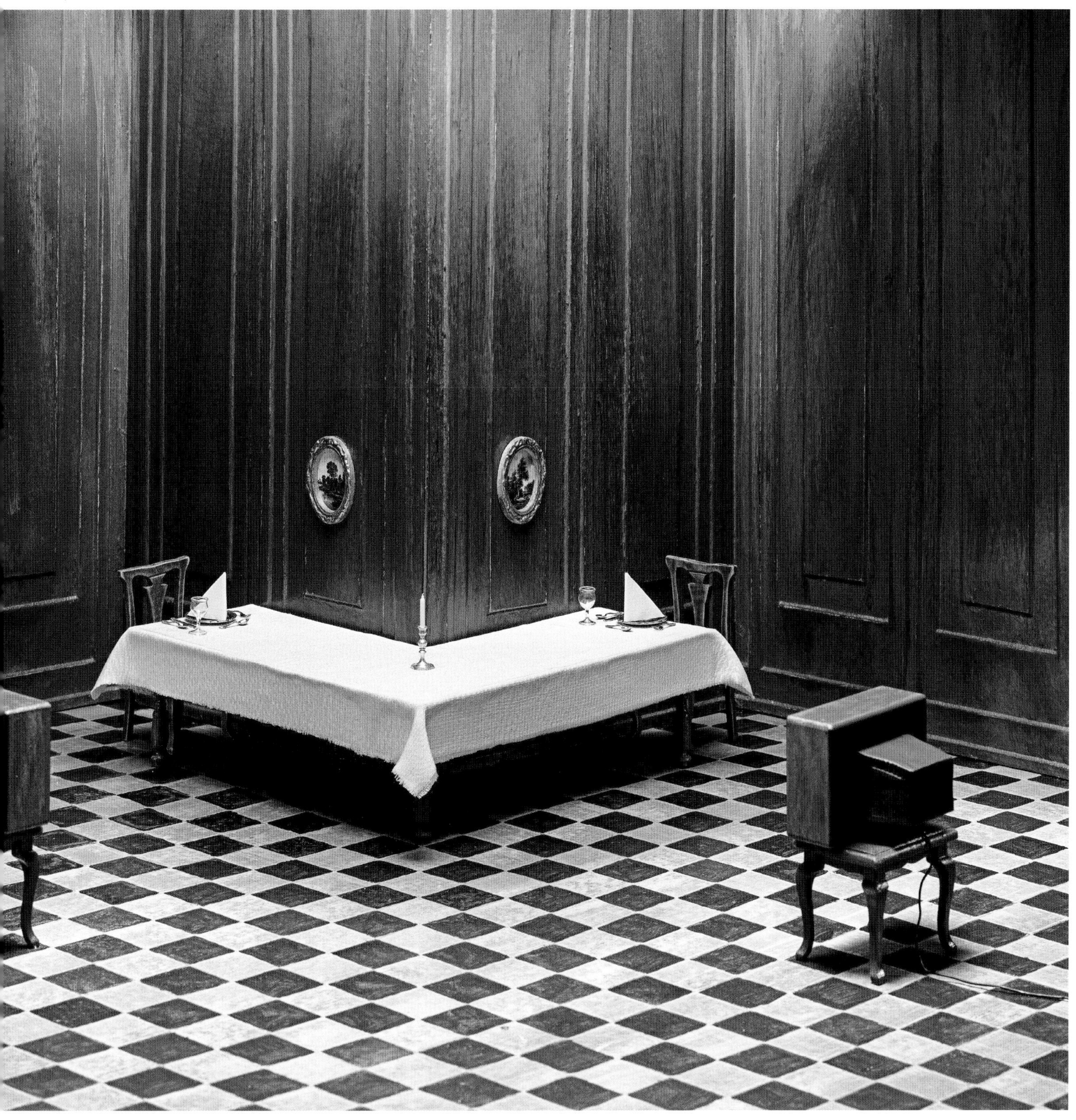

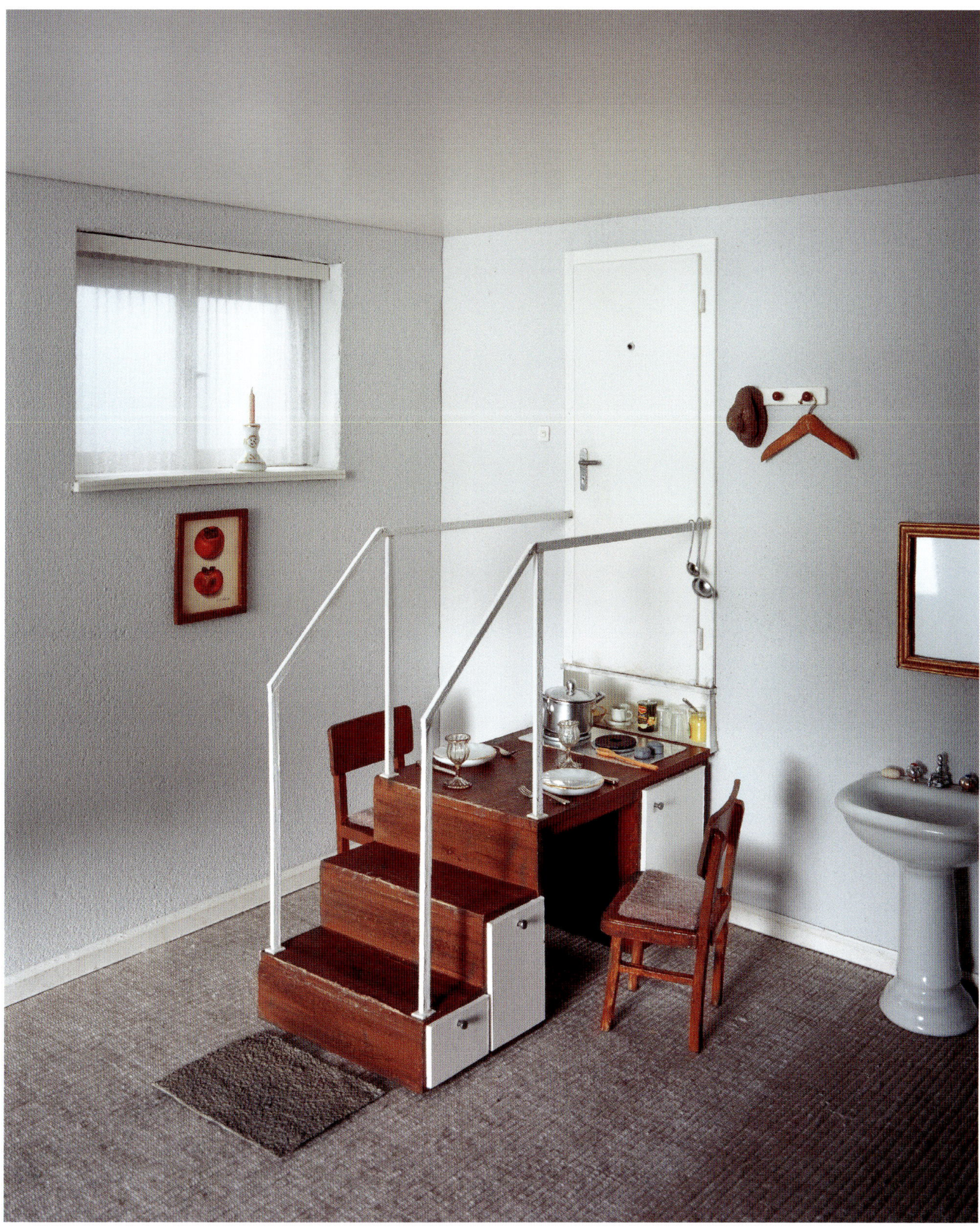

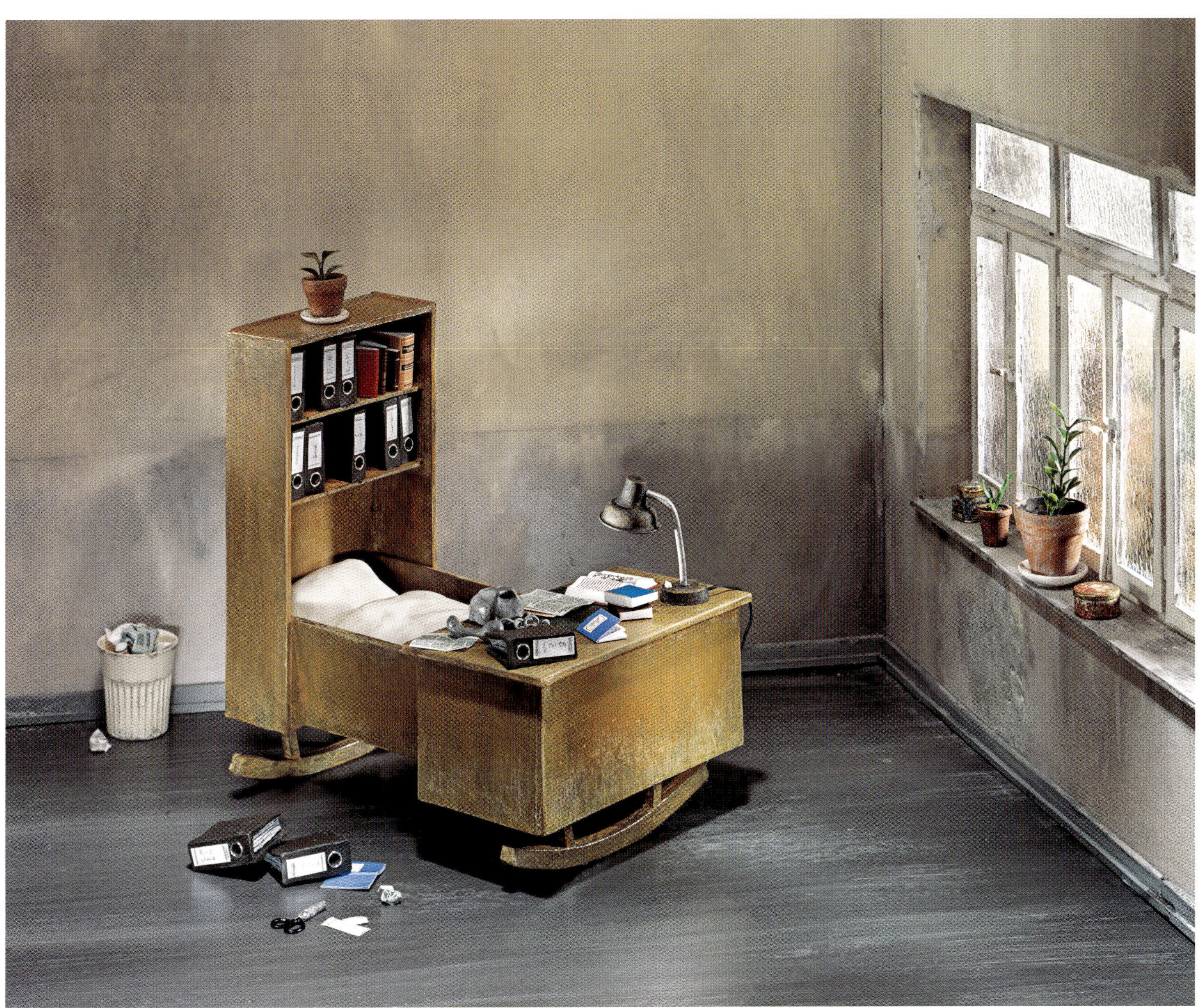

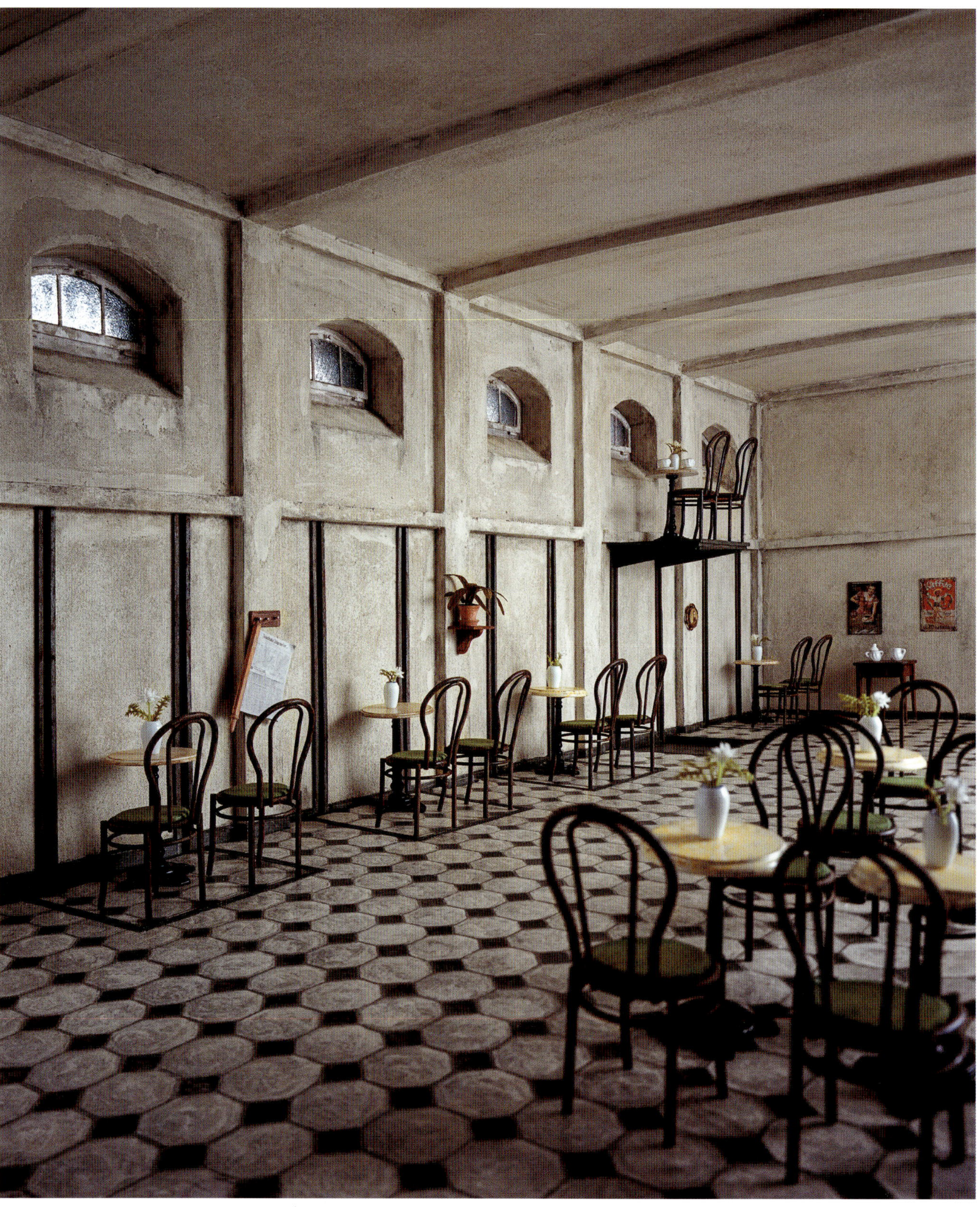

Fensterseite | Window Side
2016

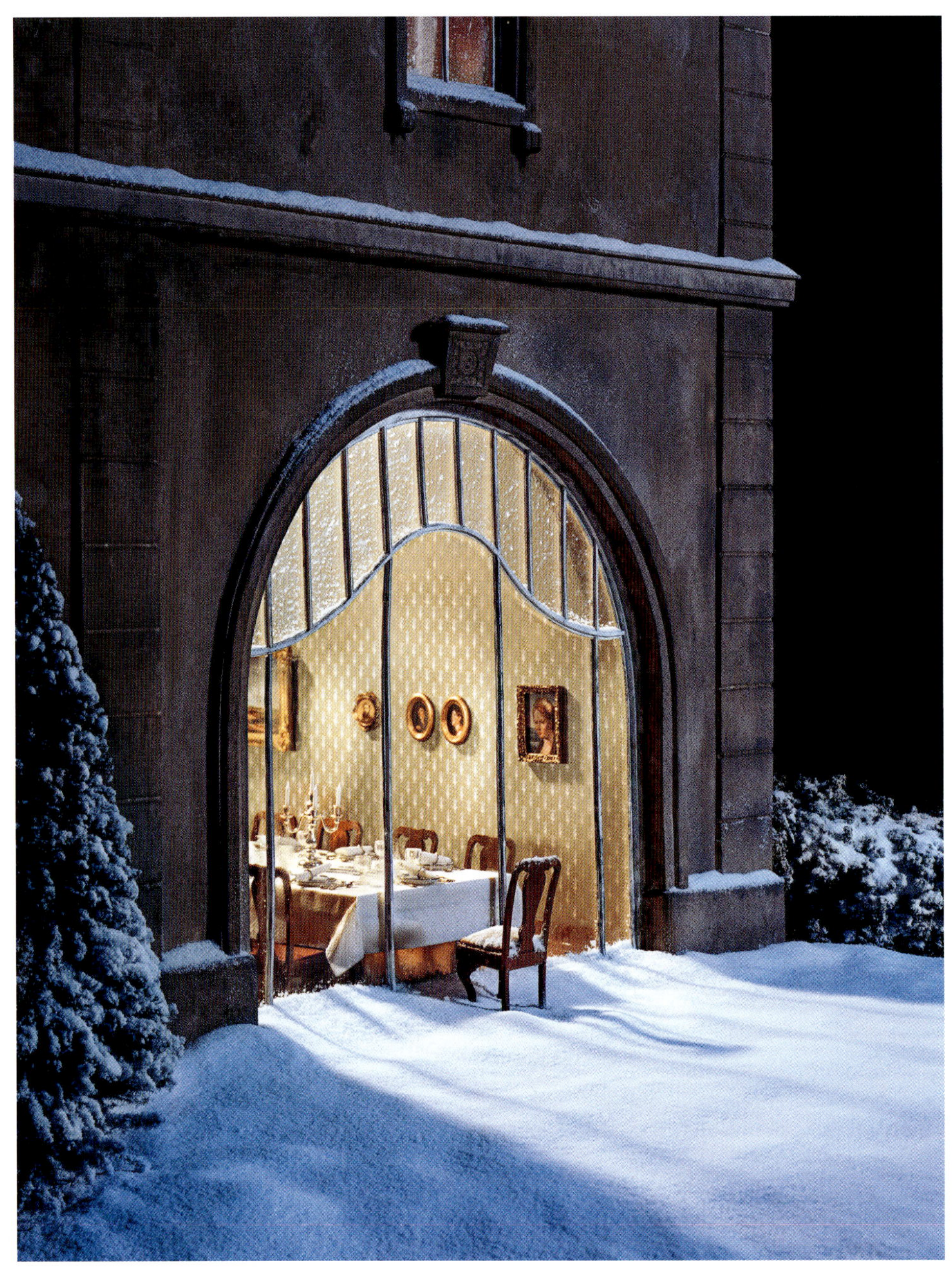

Geschlossene Gesellschaft | Private Function
2011

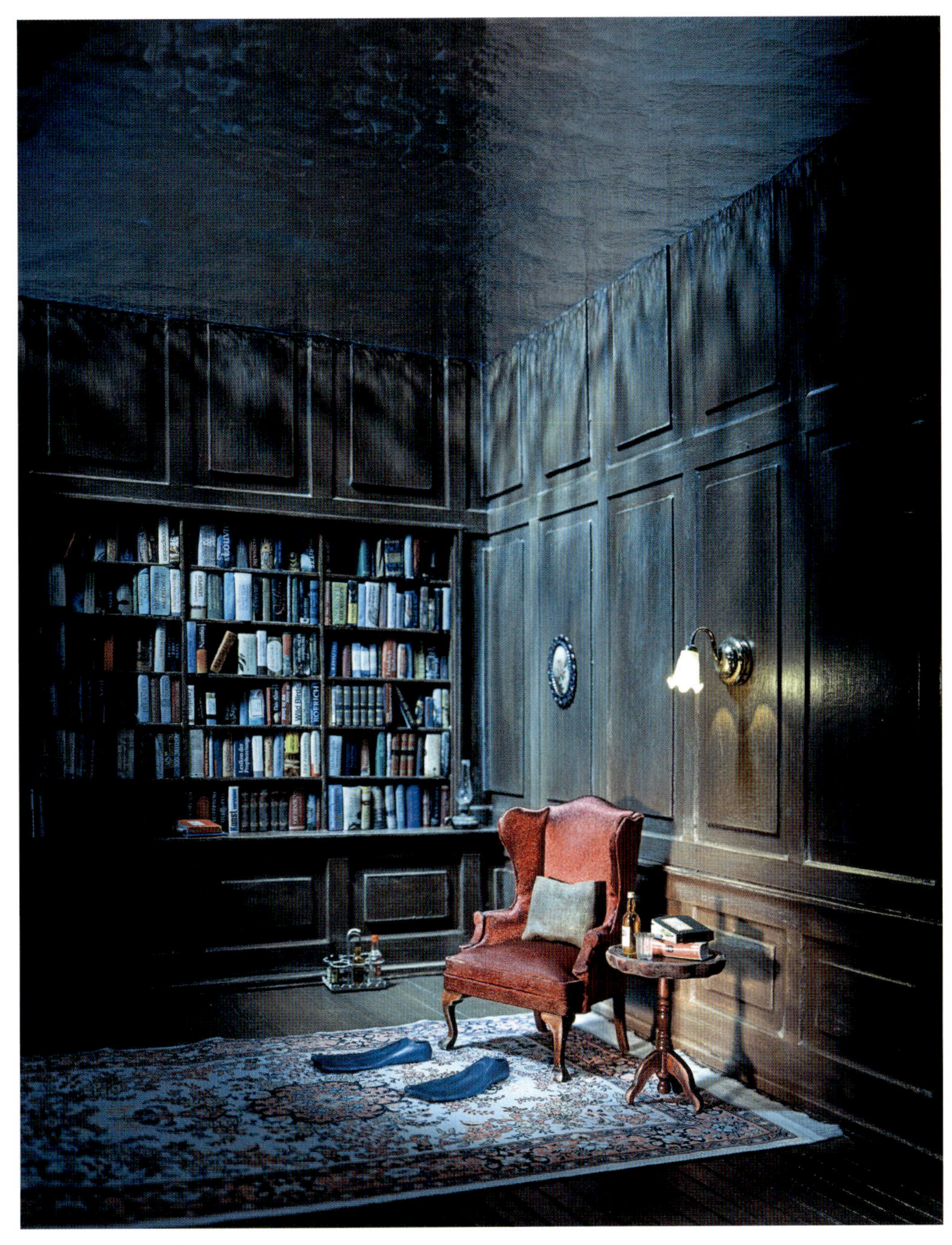

Taucherparadies | Diver's Paradise
2017

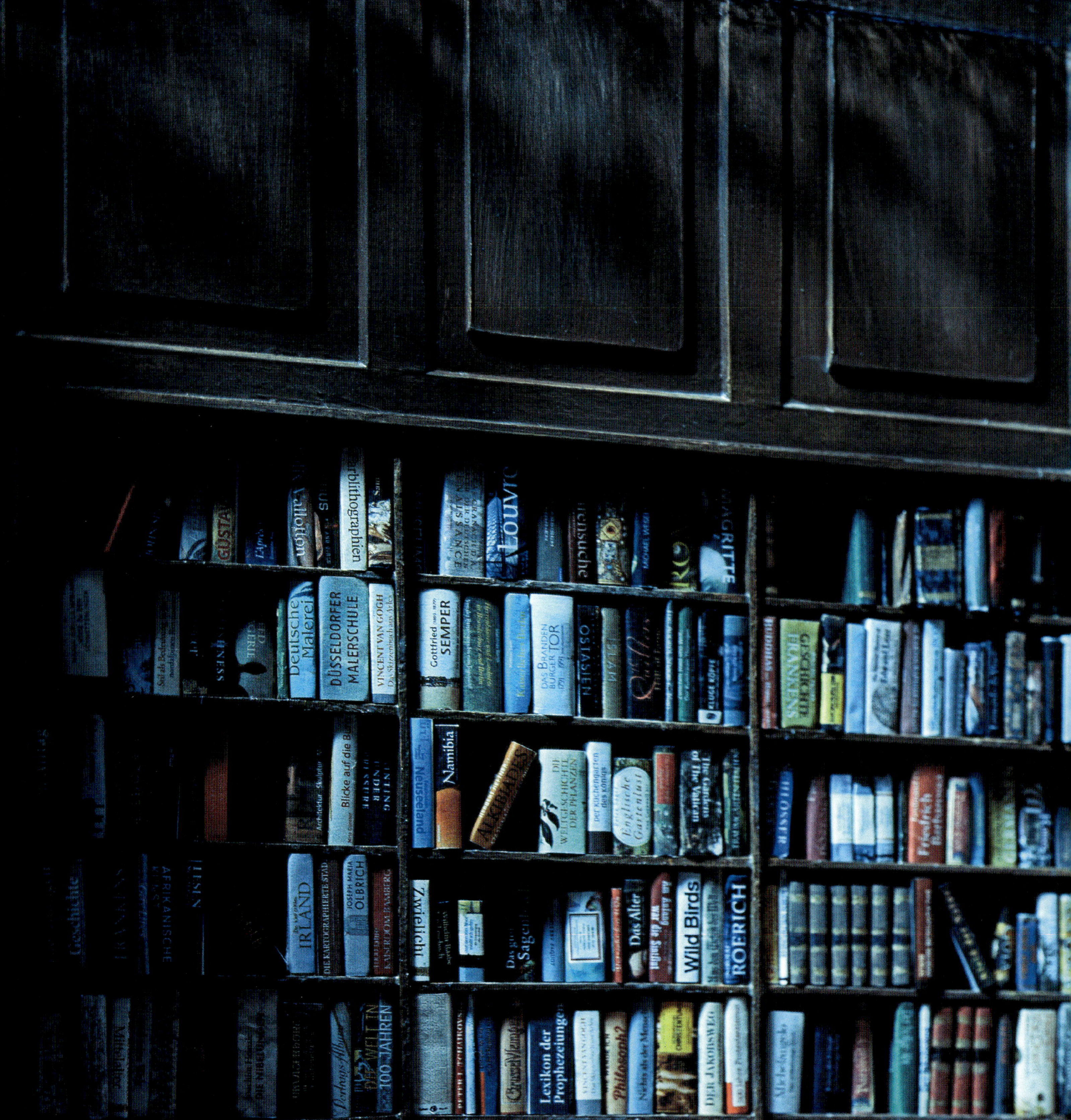
Vallotton
DÜSSELDORFER MALERSCHULE
Deutsche Malerei
VINCENT VAN GOGH
Gottfried SEMPER
DAS BRANDENBURGER TOR
MAGRITTE
Neuseeland
Namibia
ALKIBIADES
DIE WELTGESCHICHTE DER PFLANZEN
Englische Gartenlust
Blicke auf die B
IRLAND
JOSEPH MARIA OLBRICH
Zwielicht
Das Alter
Wild Birds
ROERICH
Lexikon der Prophezeiungen
Philosoph?
DER JAKOBSWEG
100 JAHREN
Friedrich

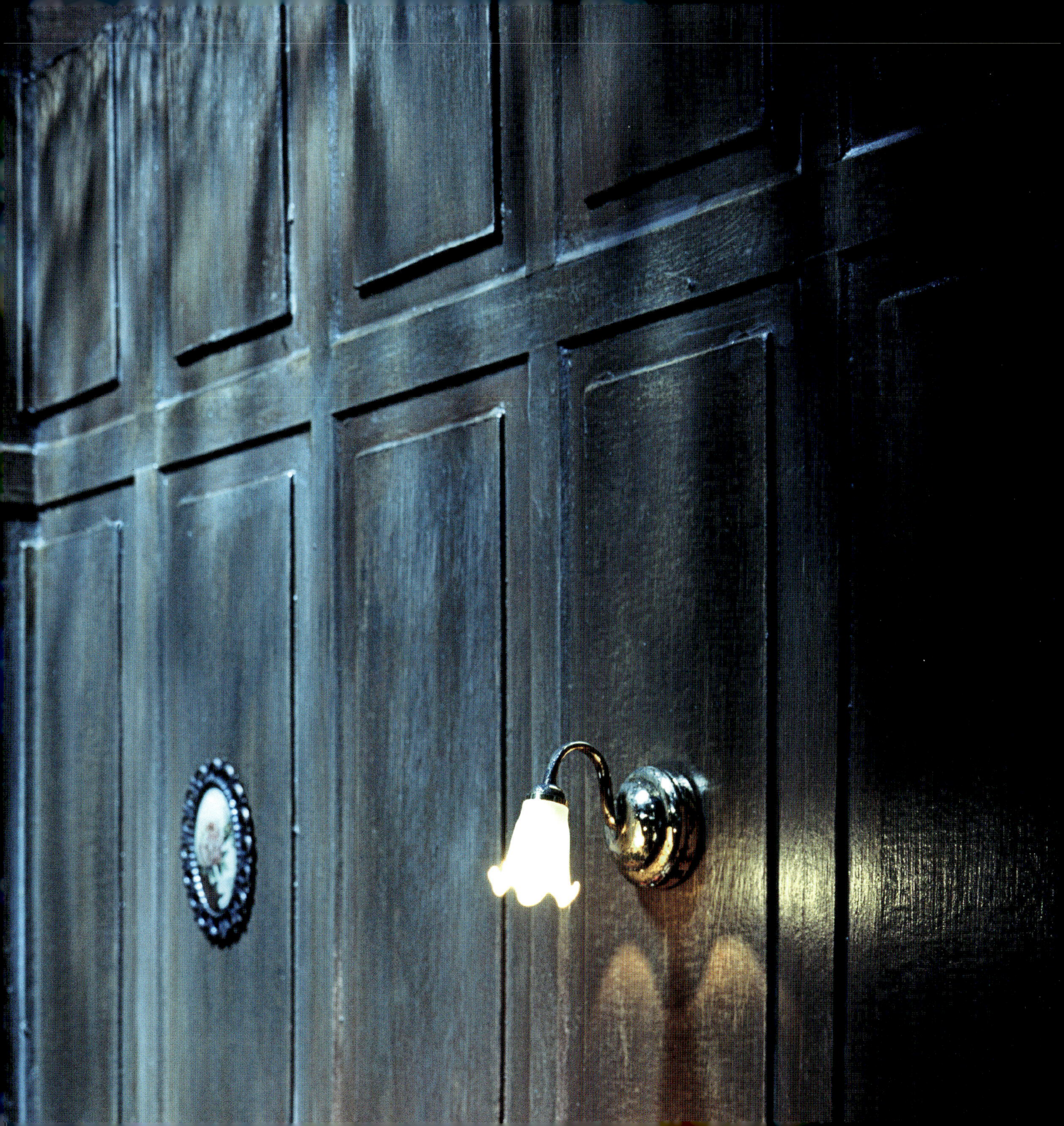

Im Rausch der Tiefe | The Depths of Ecstasy
2002

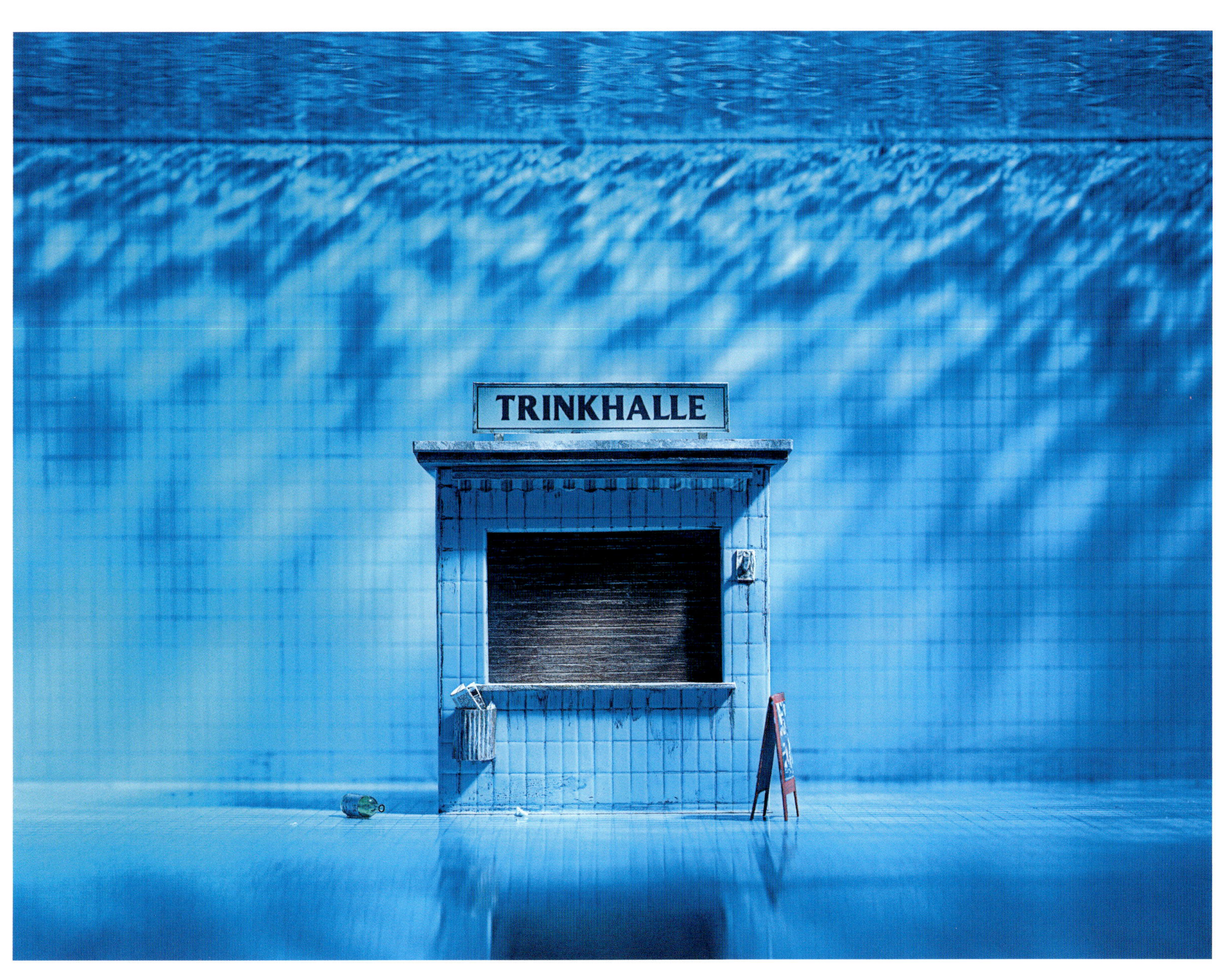
TRINKHALLE

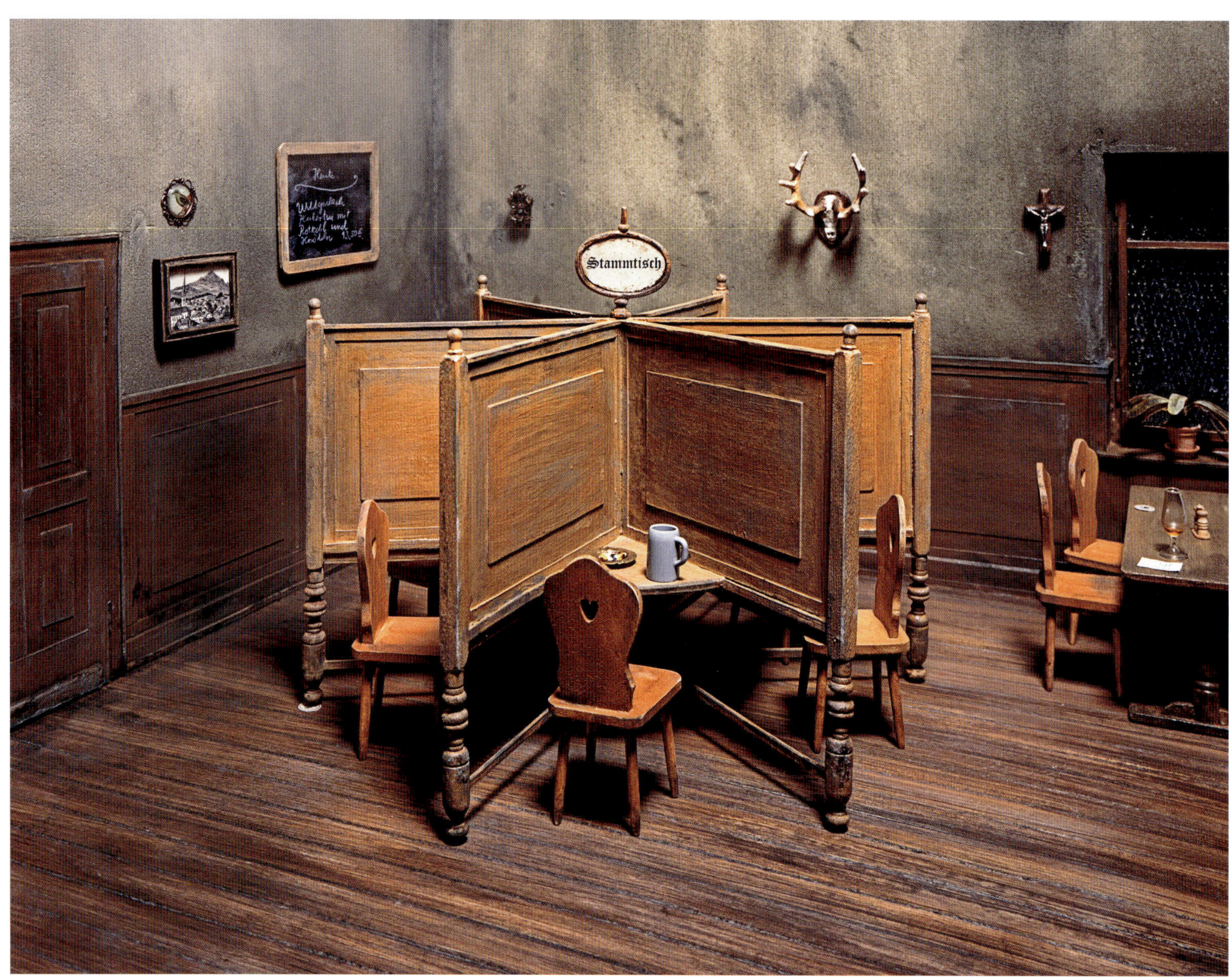
Stammtisch

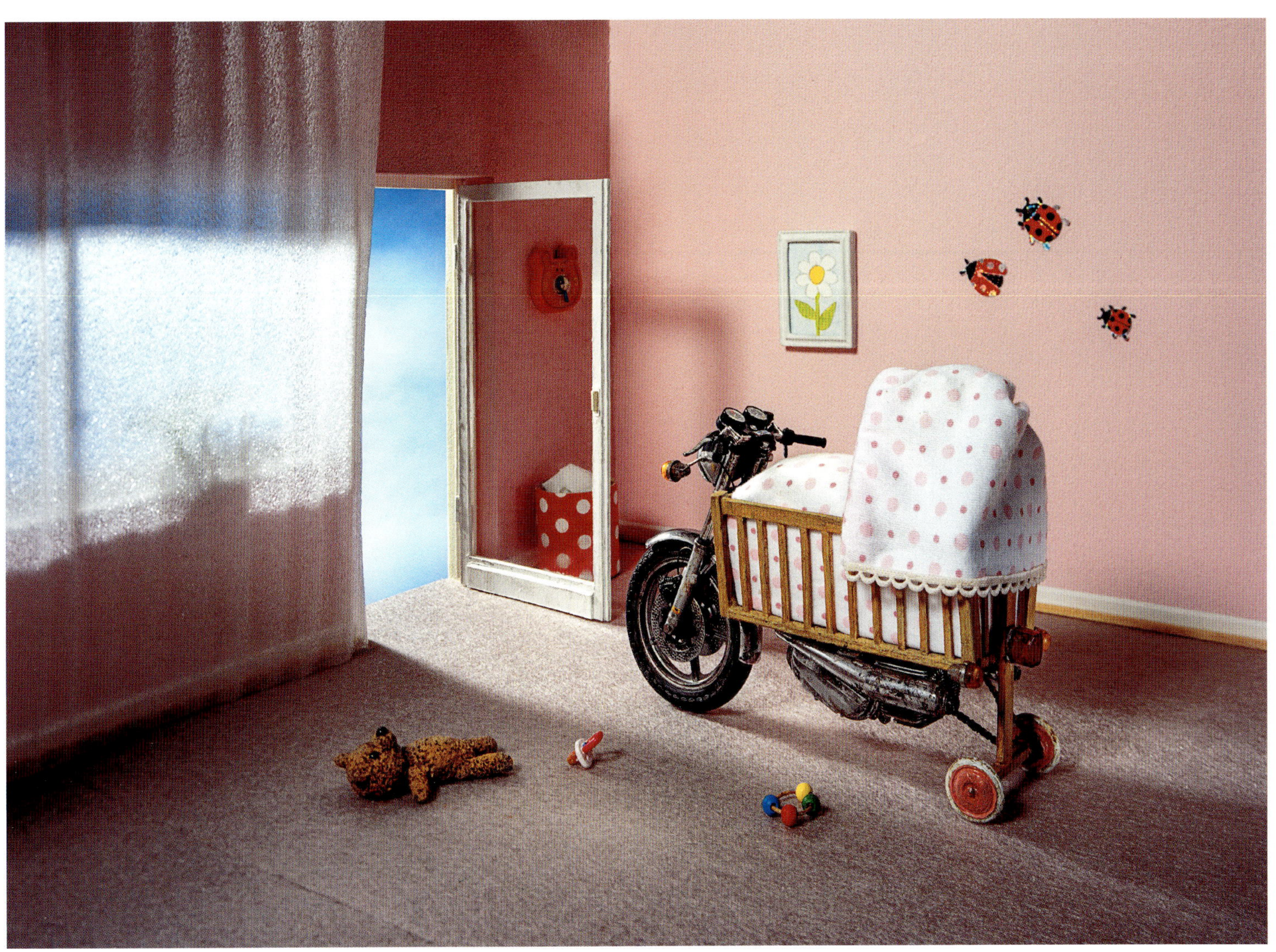

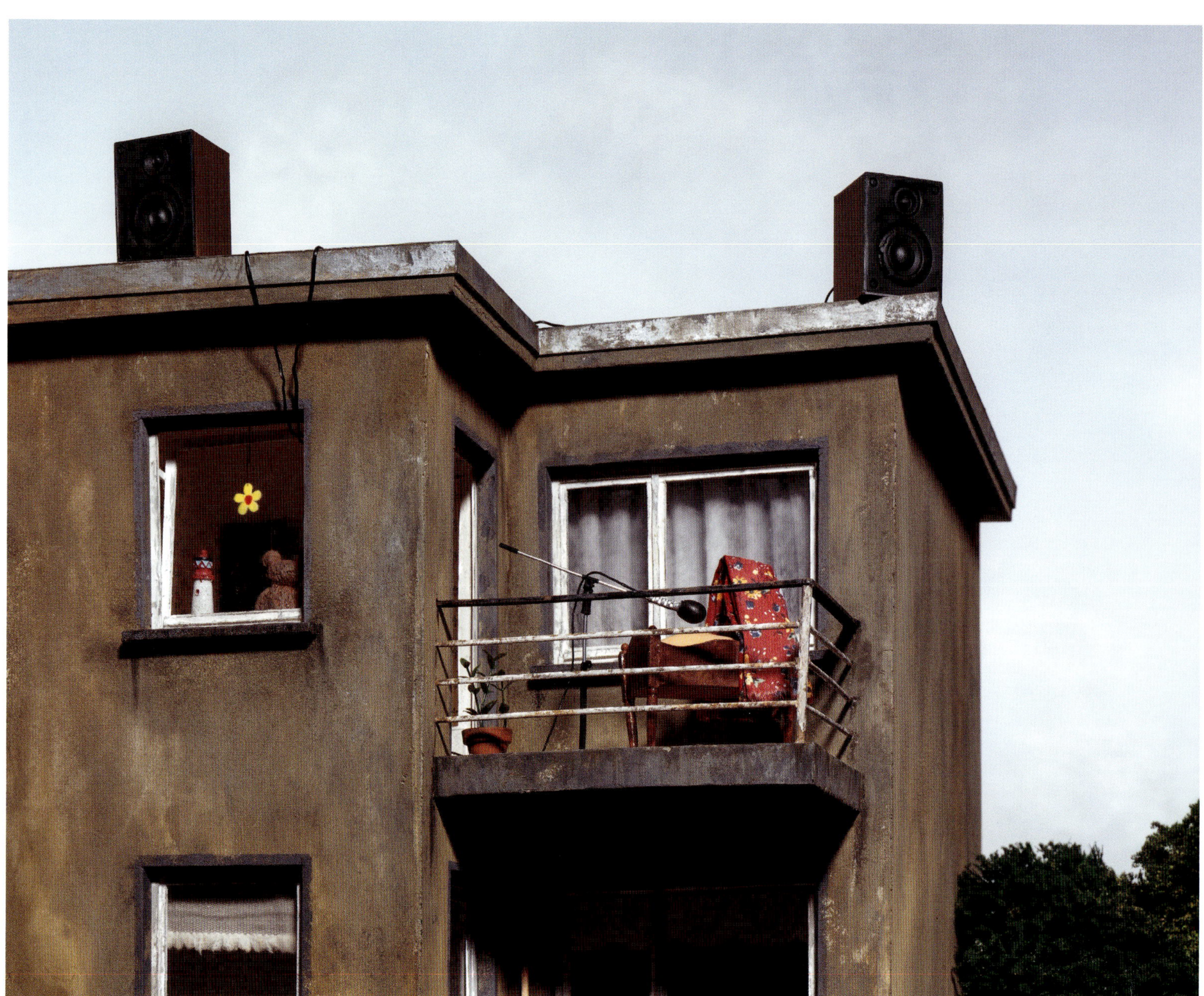

Babyfon | Baby Monitor
2011

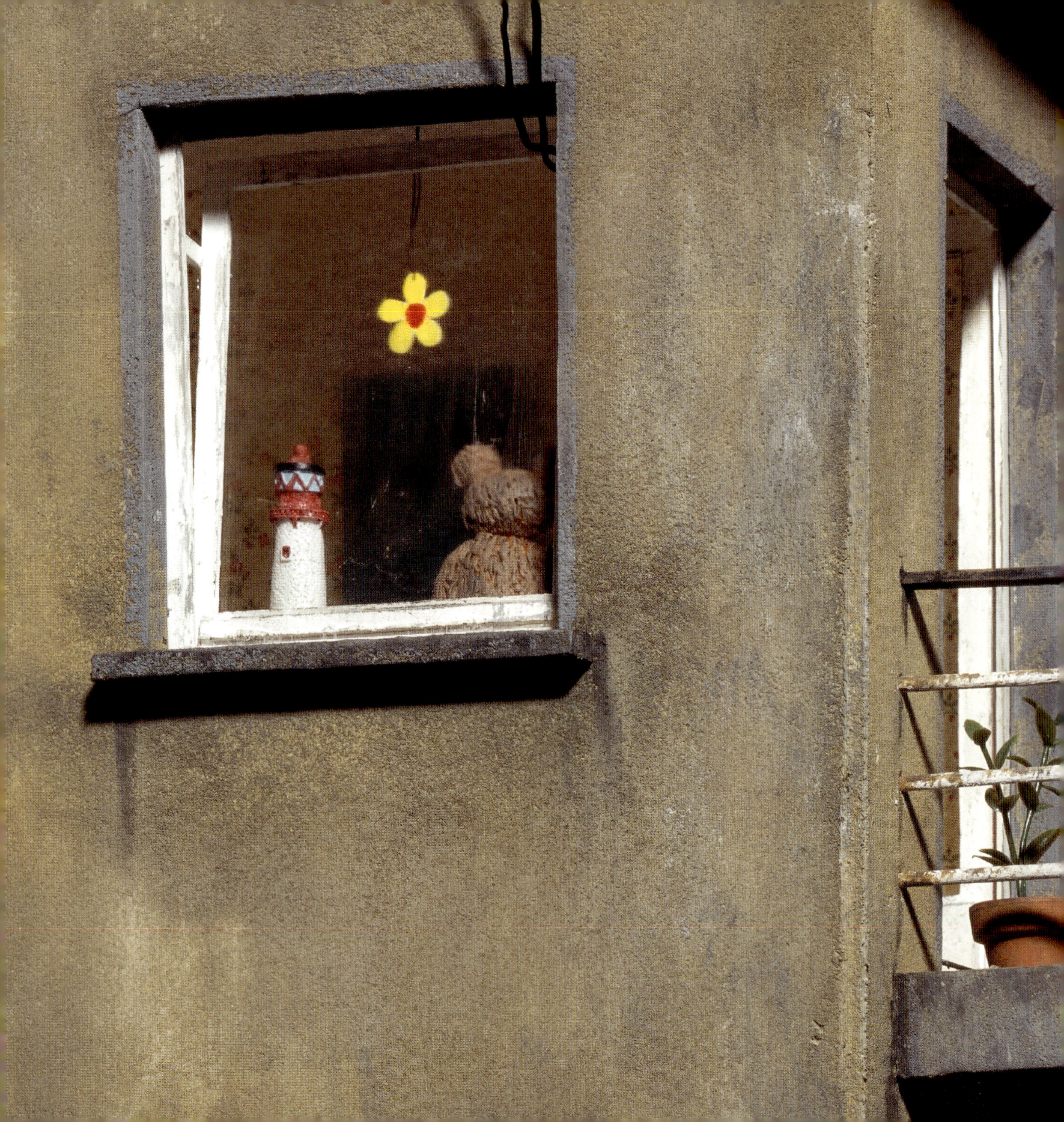

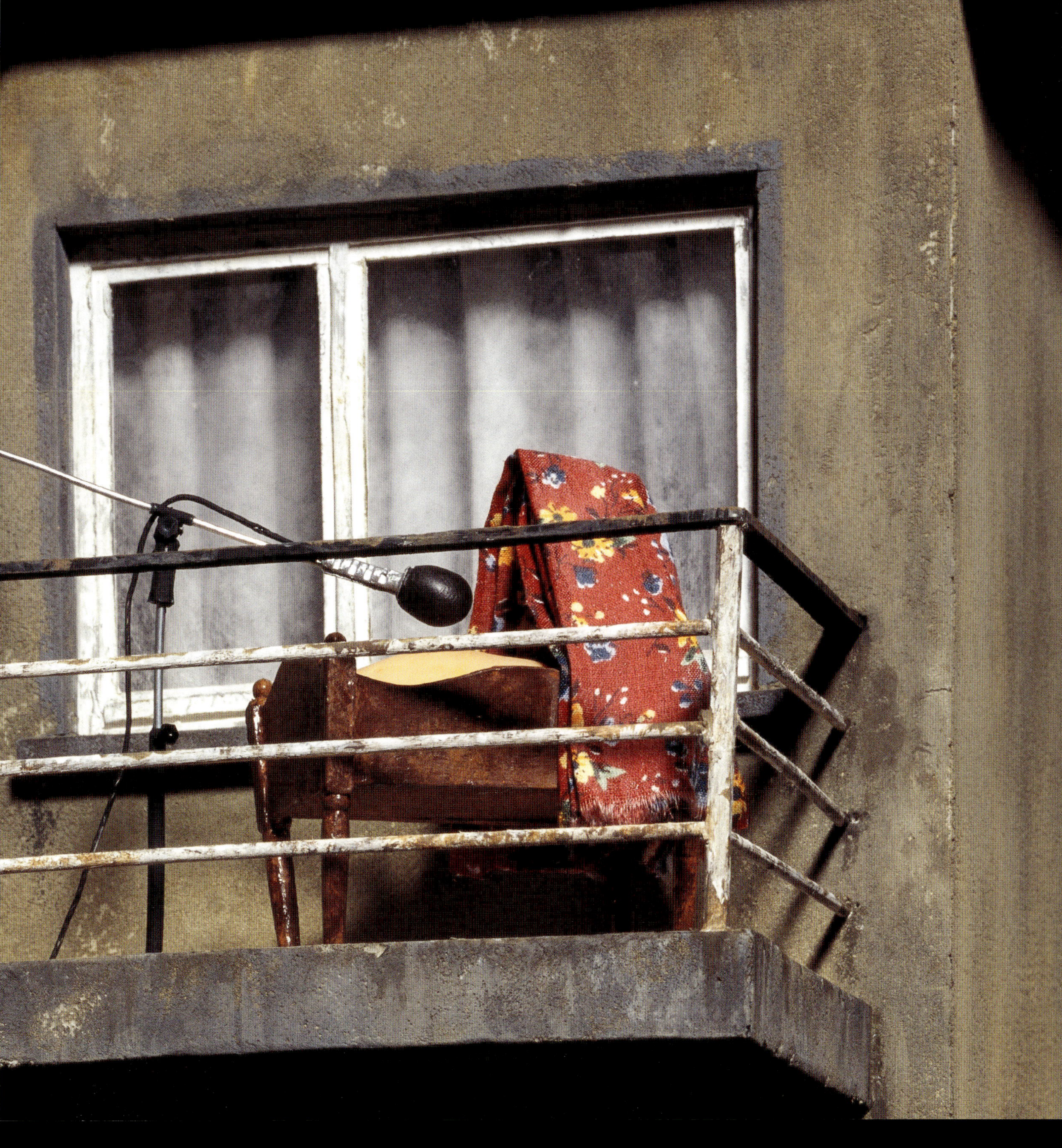

Sonnenseite | Sunny Side
2004

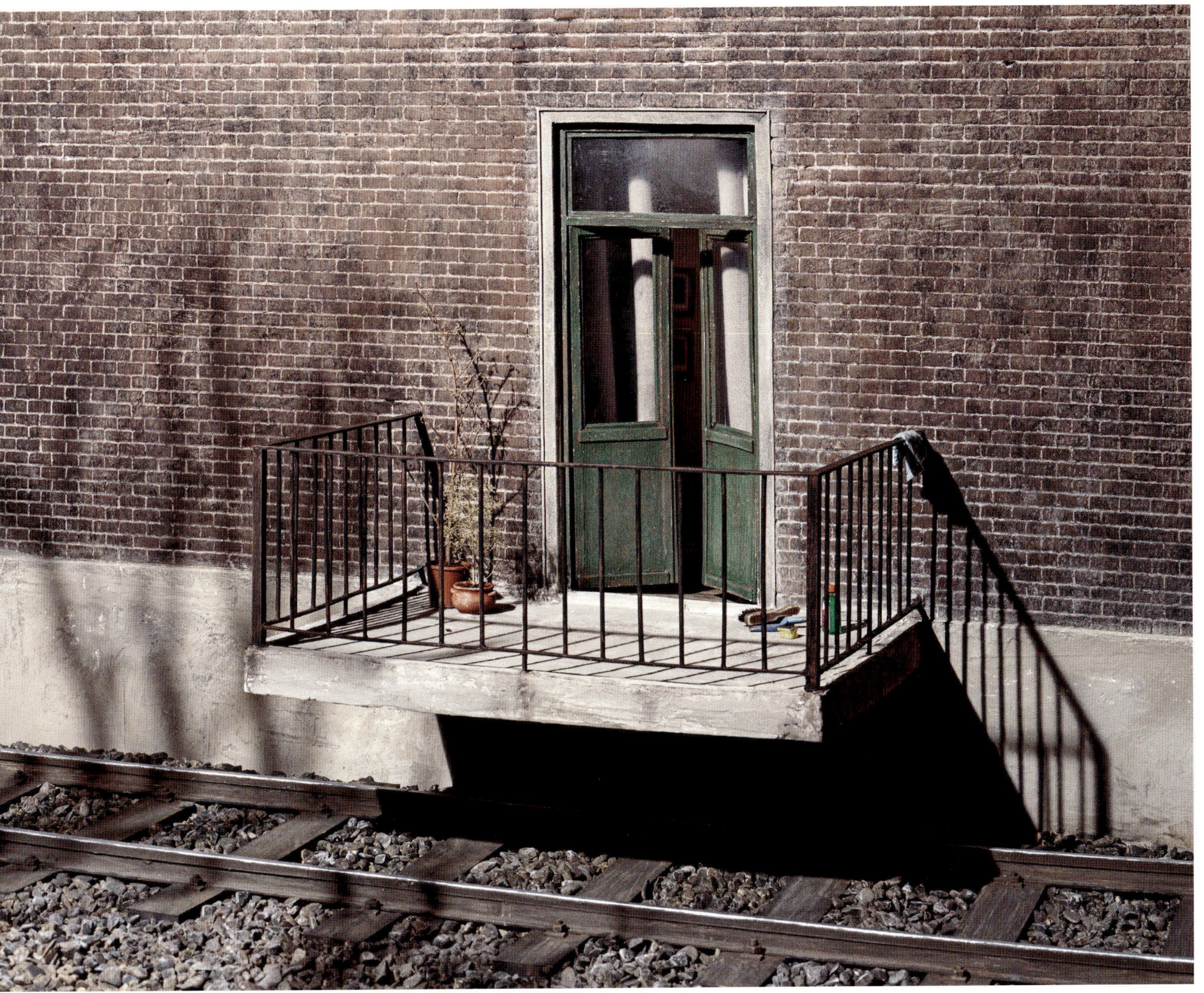

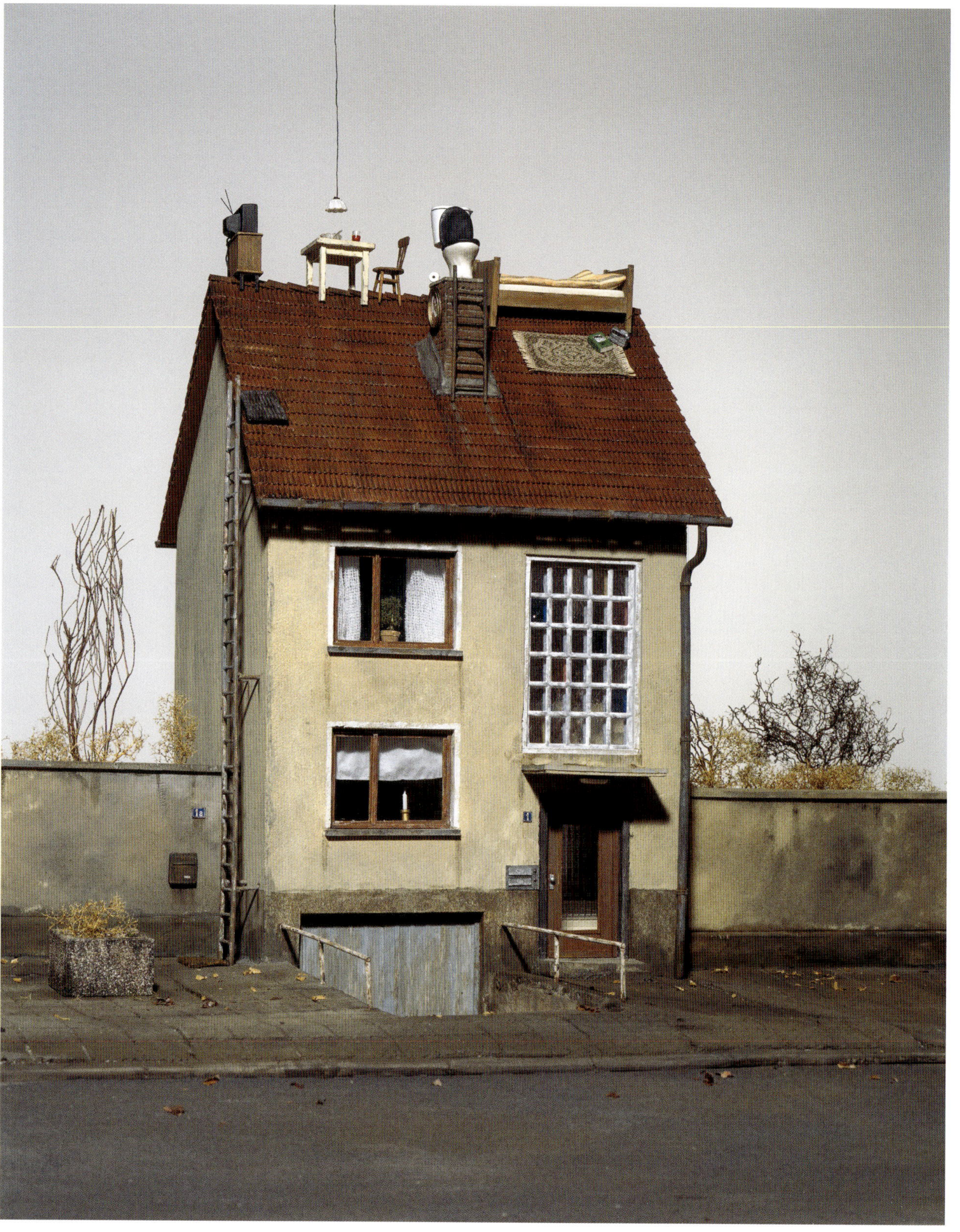

Dachwohnung | Attic Flat
2007

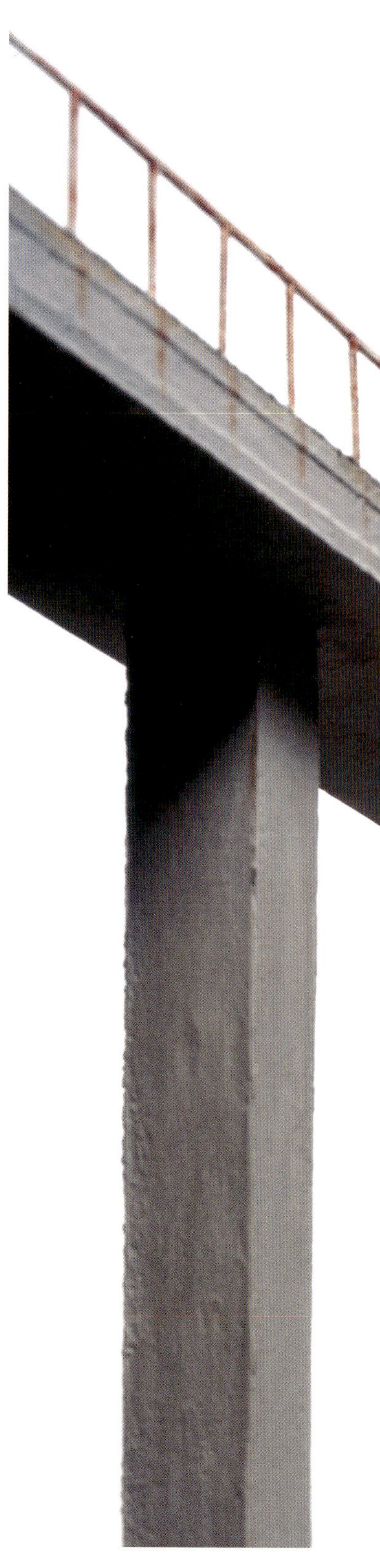

Dem Himmel so nah | Almost Heavenly
2002

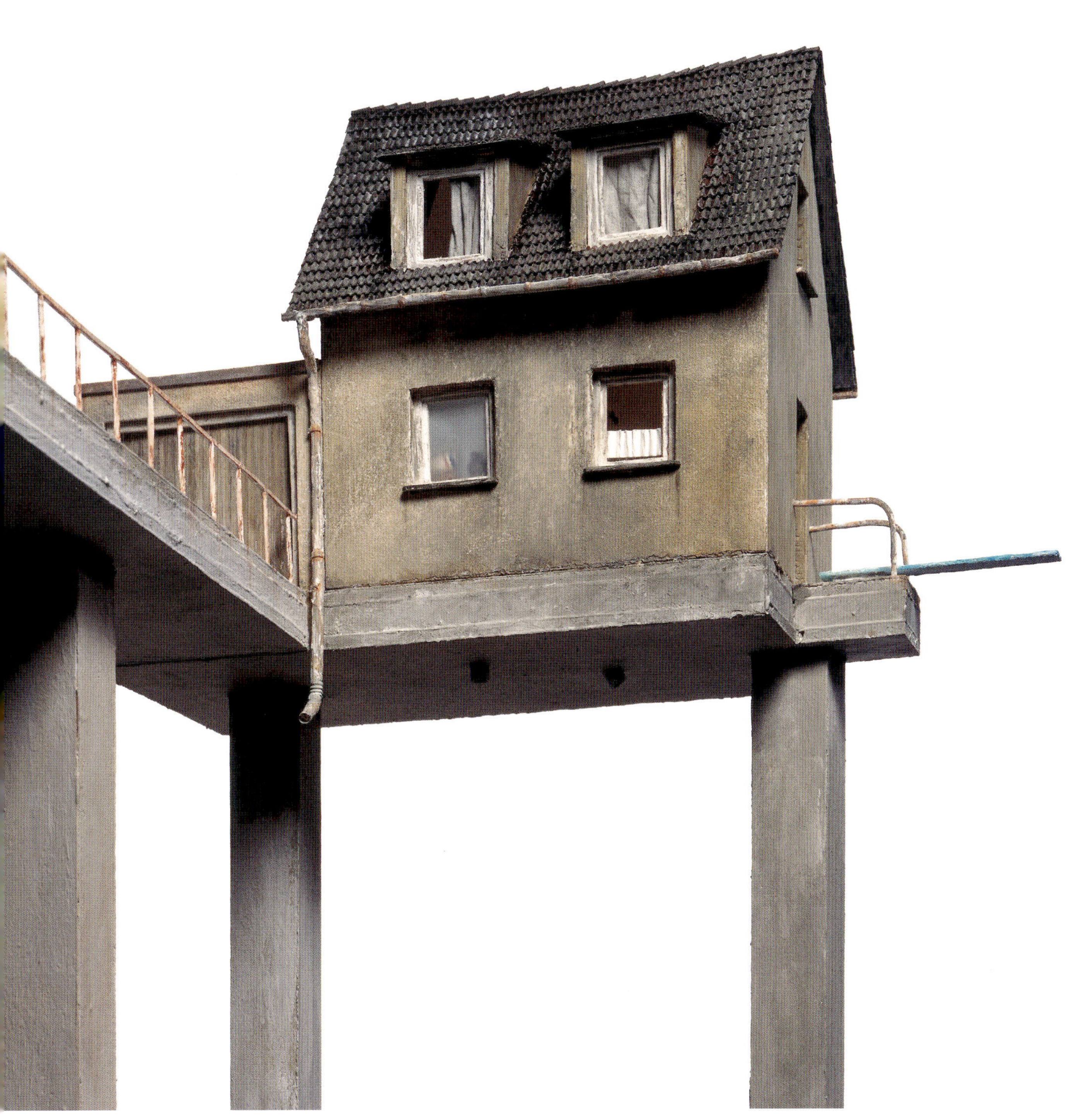

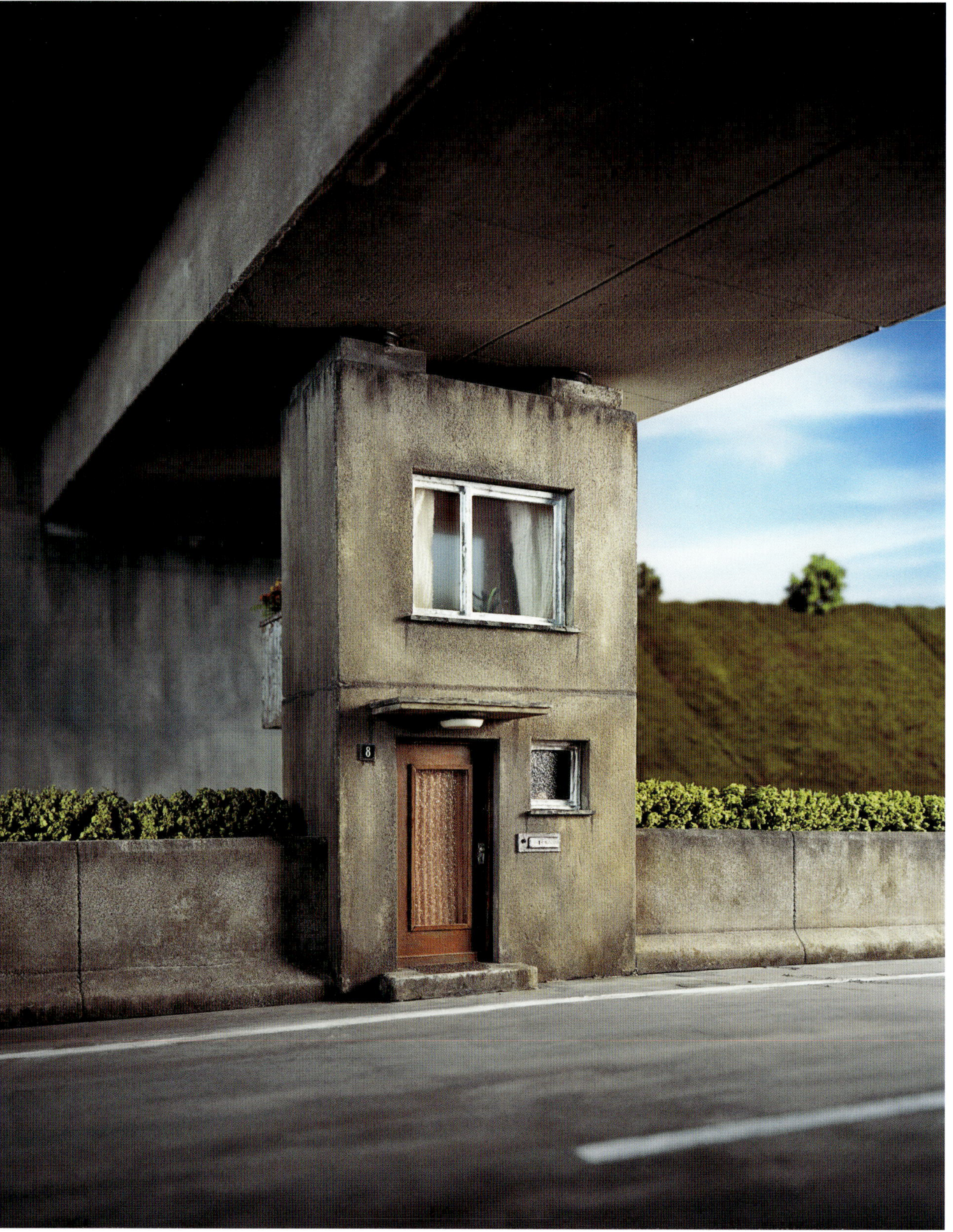
8

Unter der Brücke | Under the Bridge
2016

Mit Balkon | With Balcony
2002

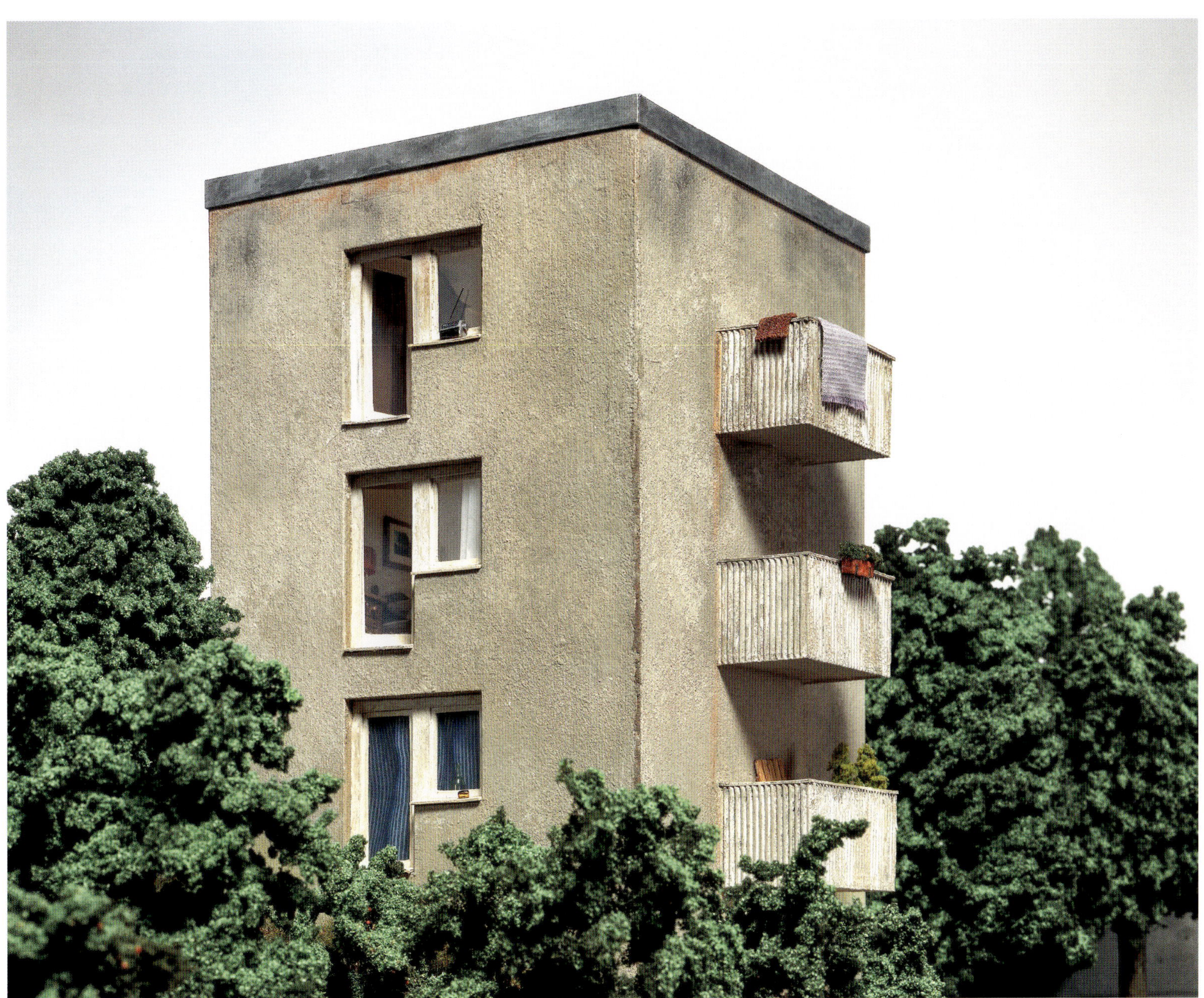

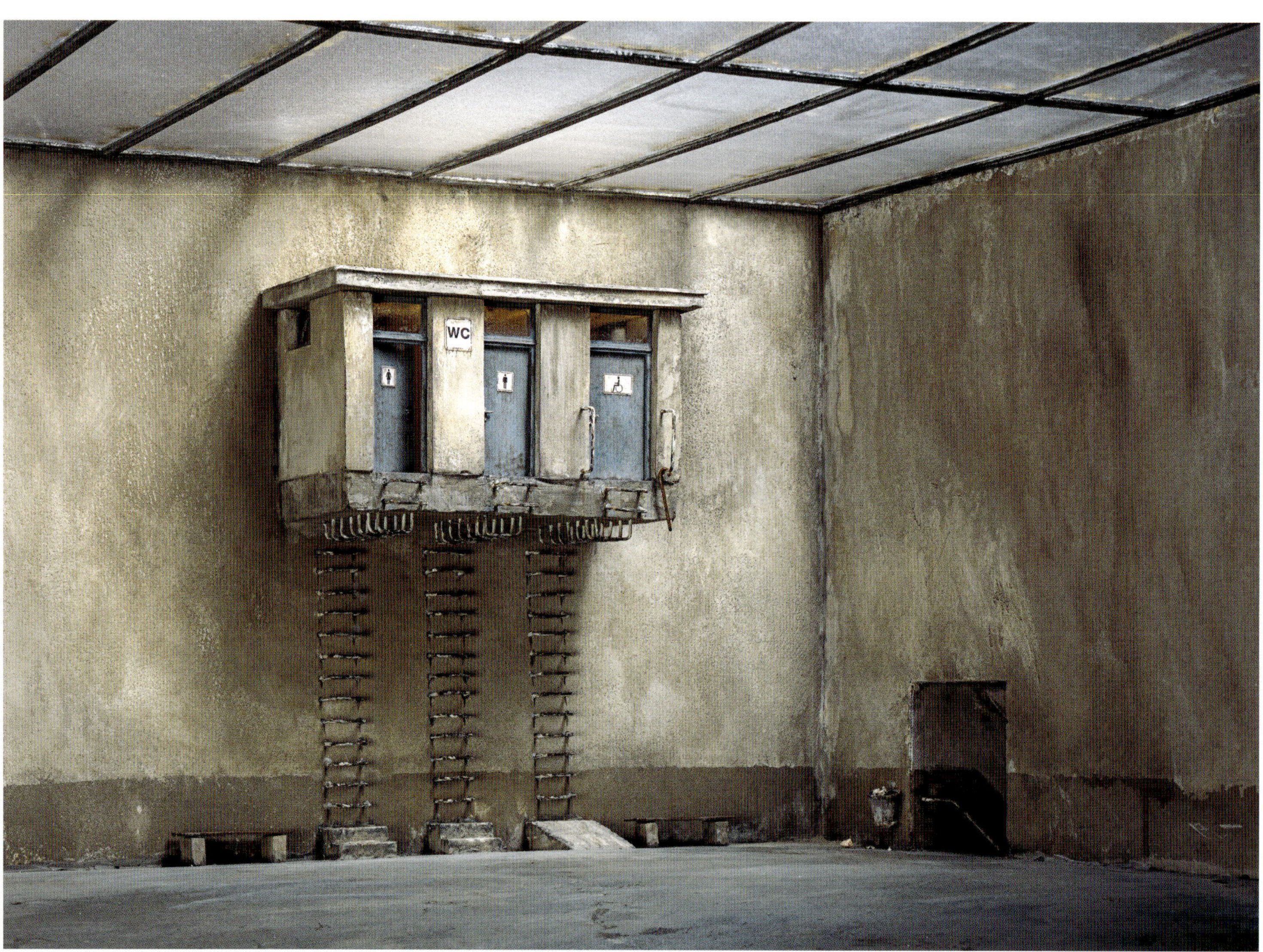
WC

WC im OG | Upstairs Toilet
2010

Streichelzoo | Petting Zoo
2001

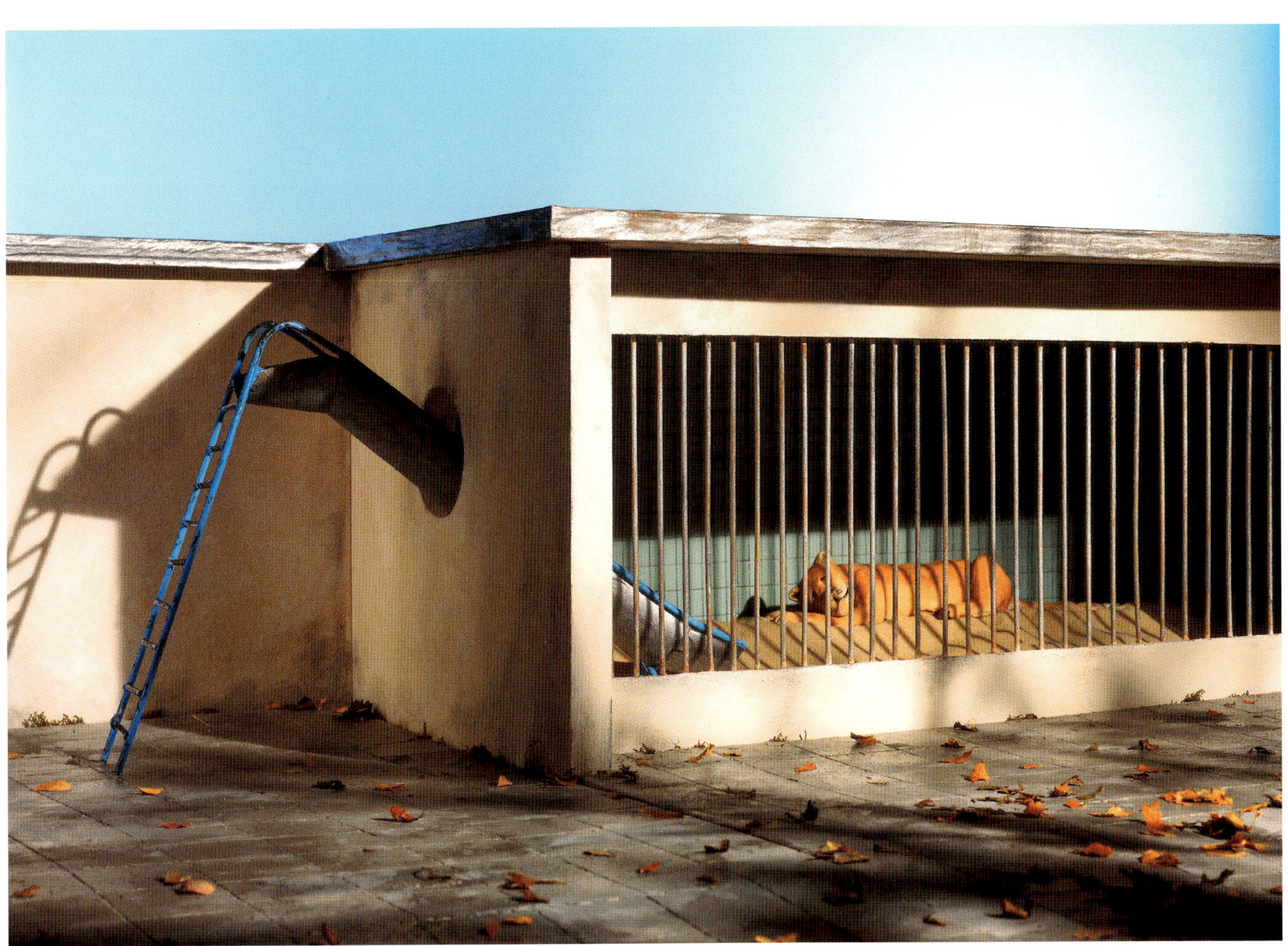

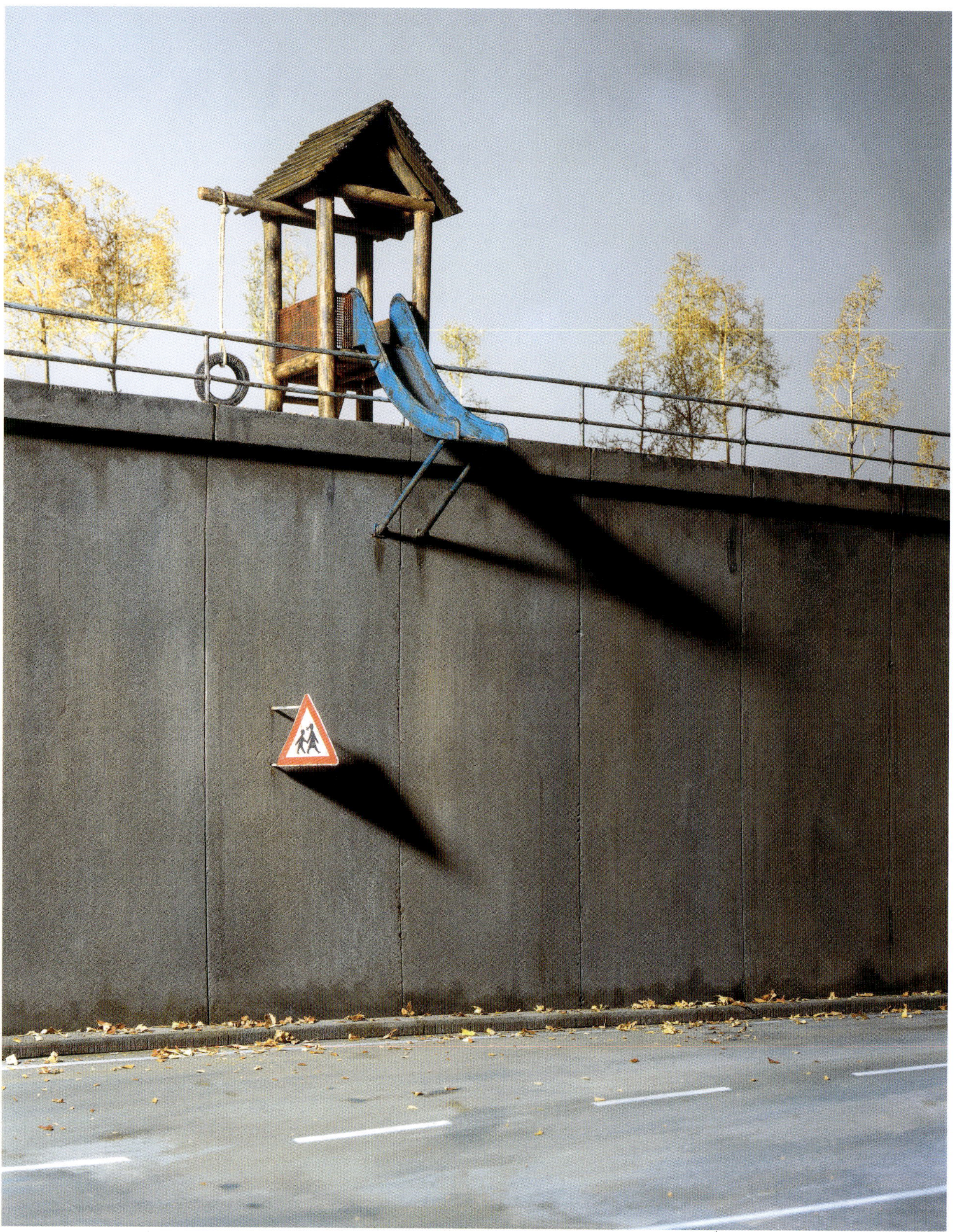

Kinder! | Children!
2006

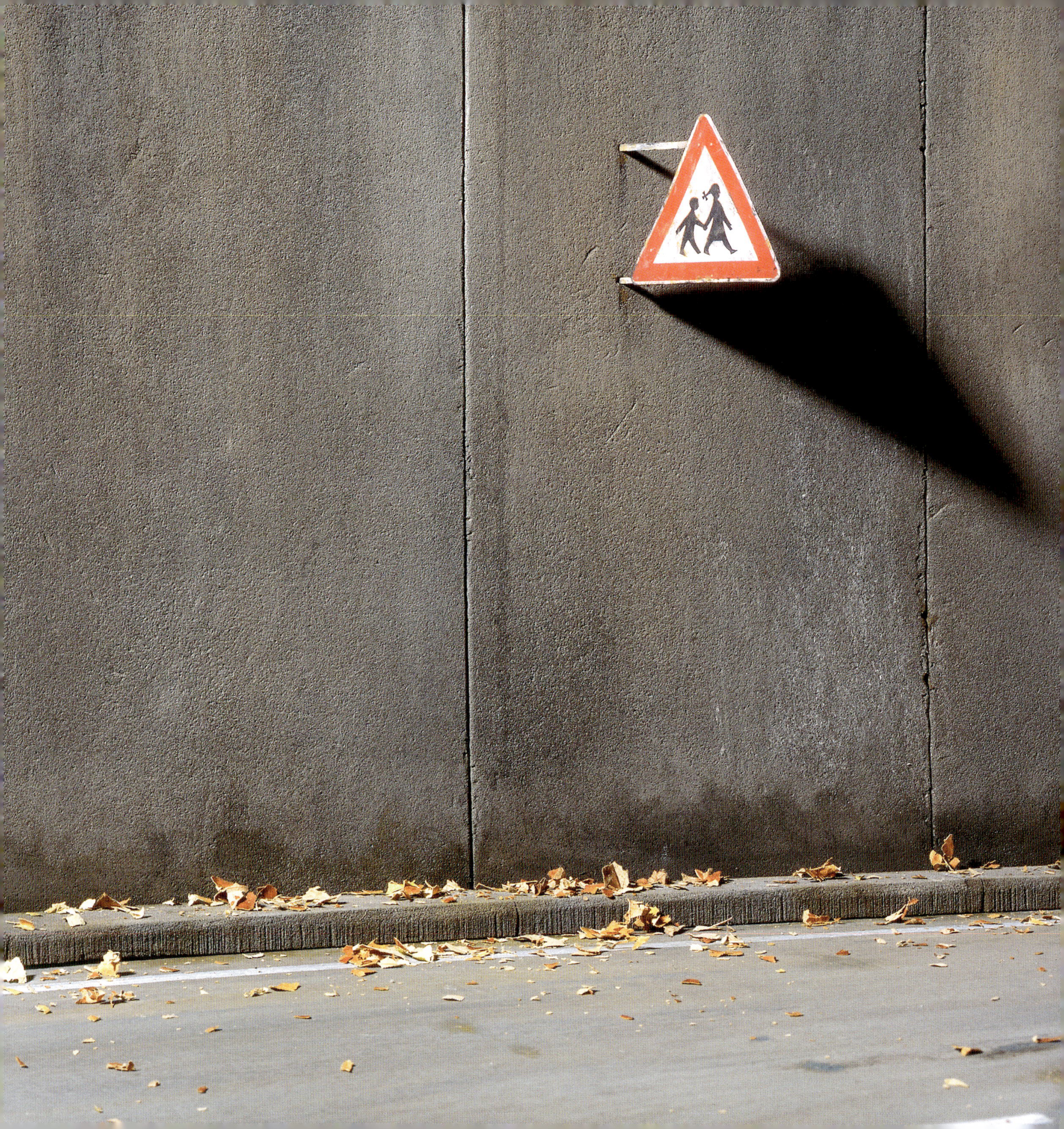

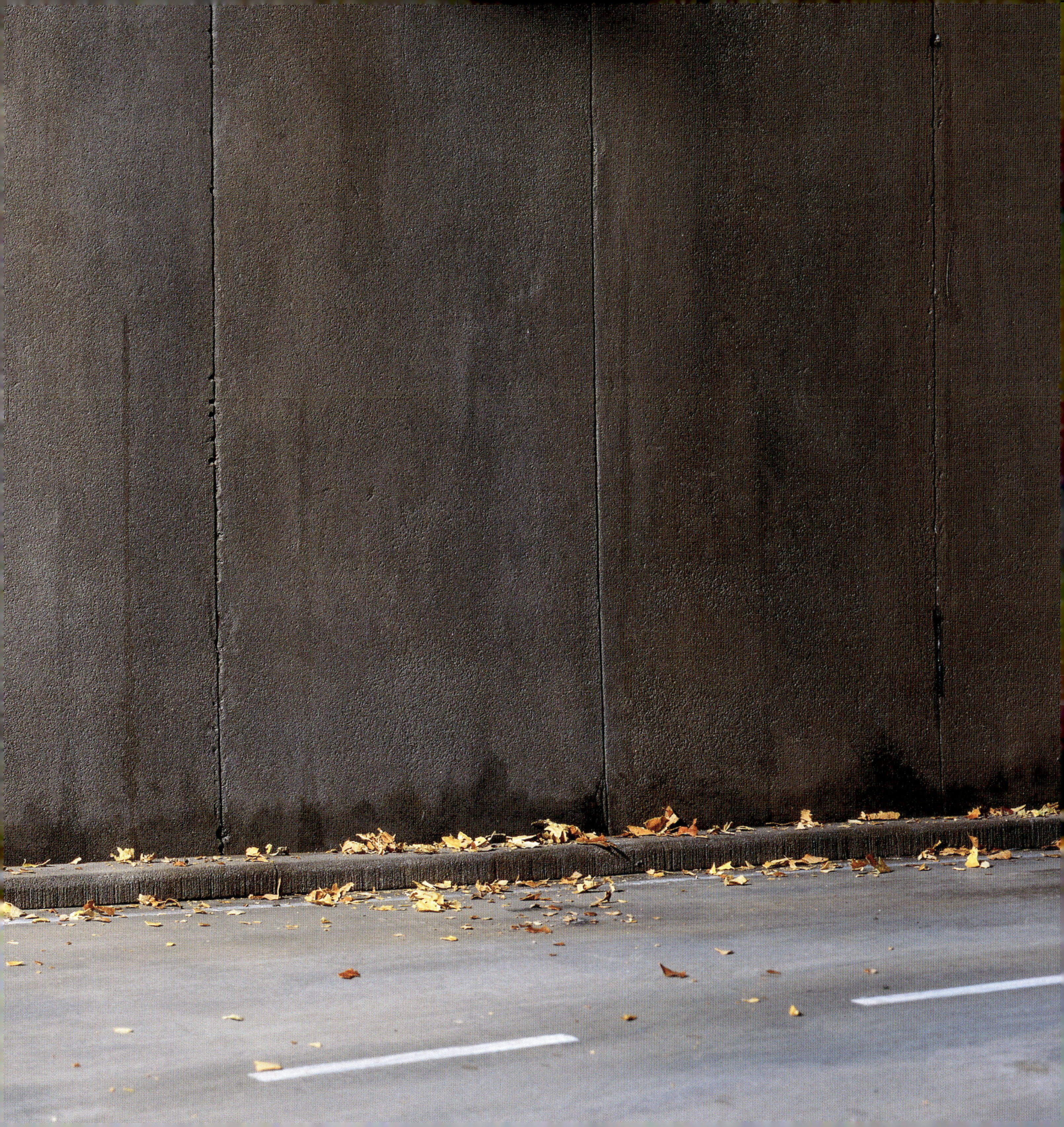

Erlebnisbad | Adventure Pool Complex
2004

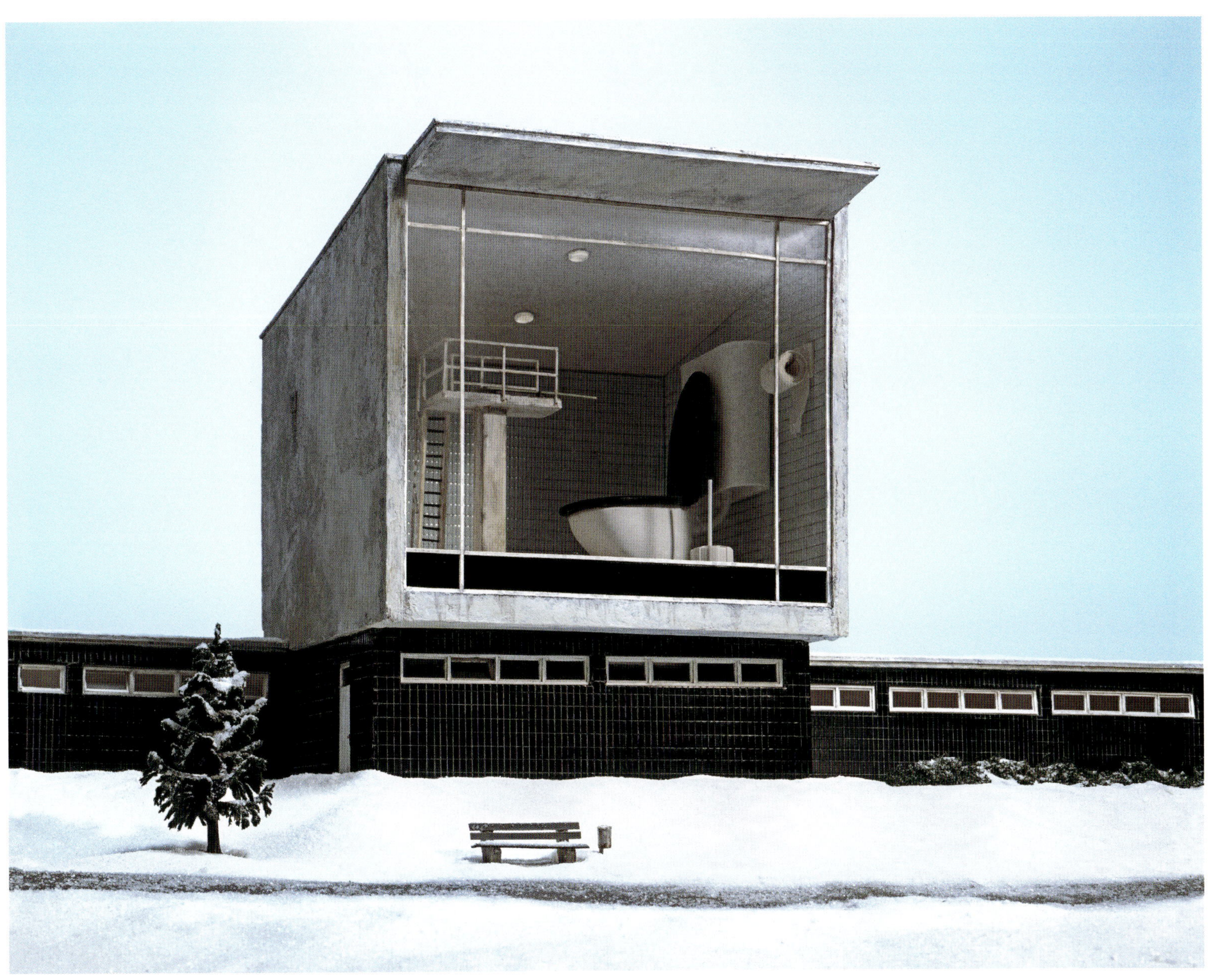

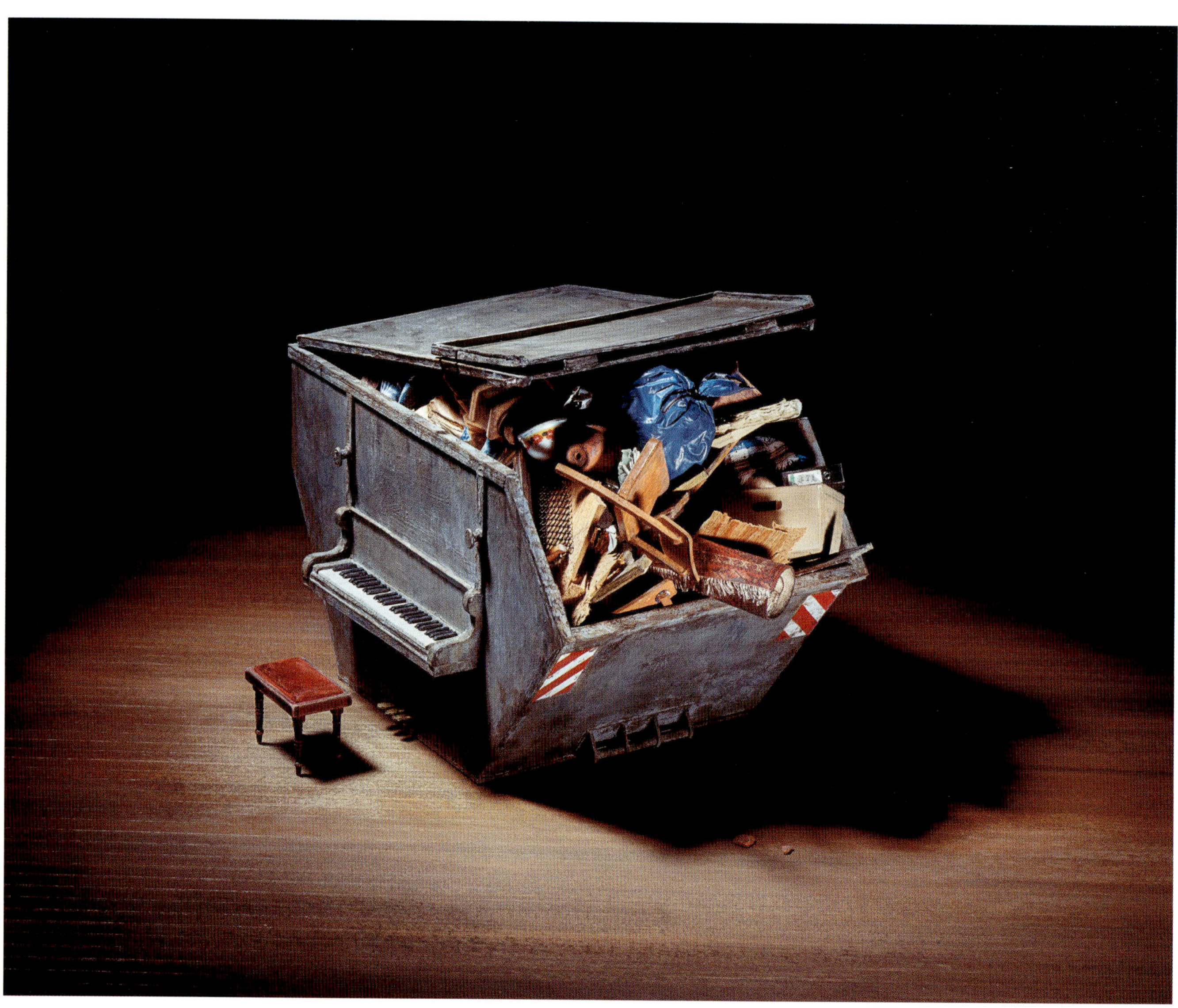

Trash
2015

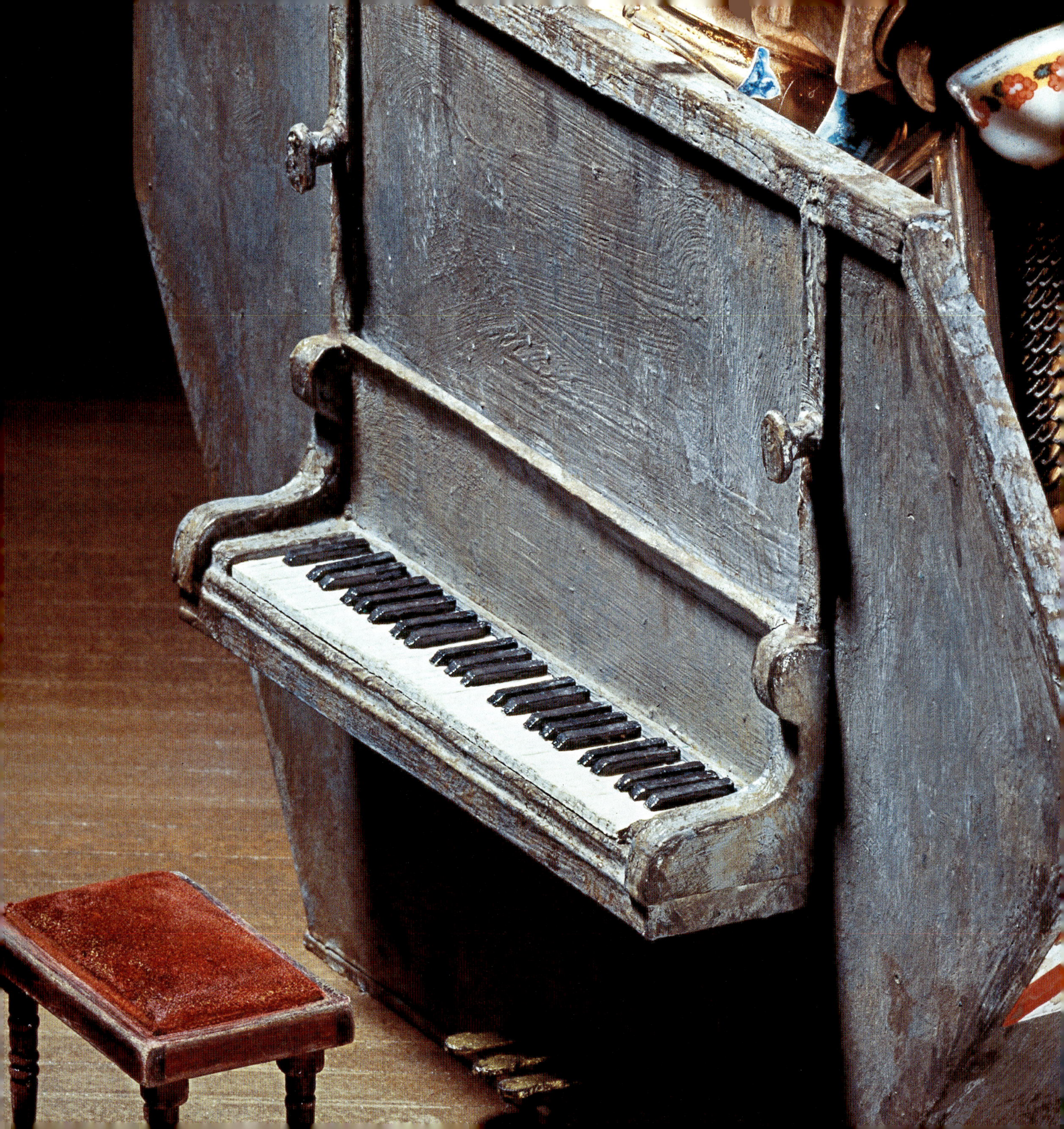

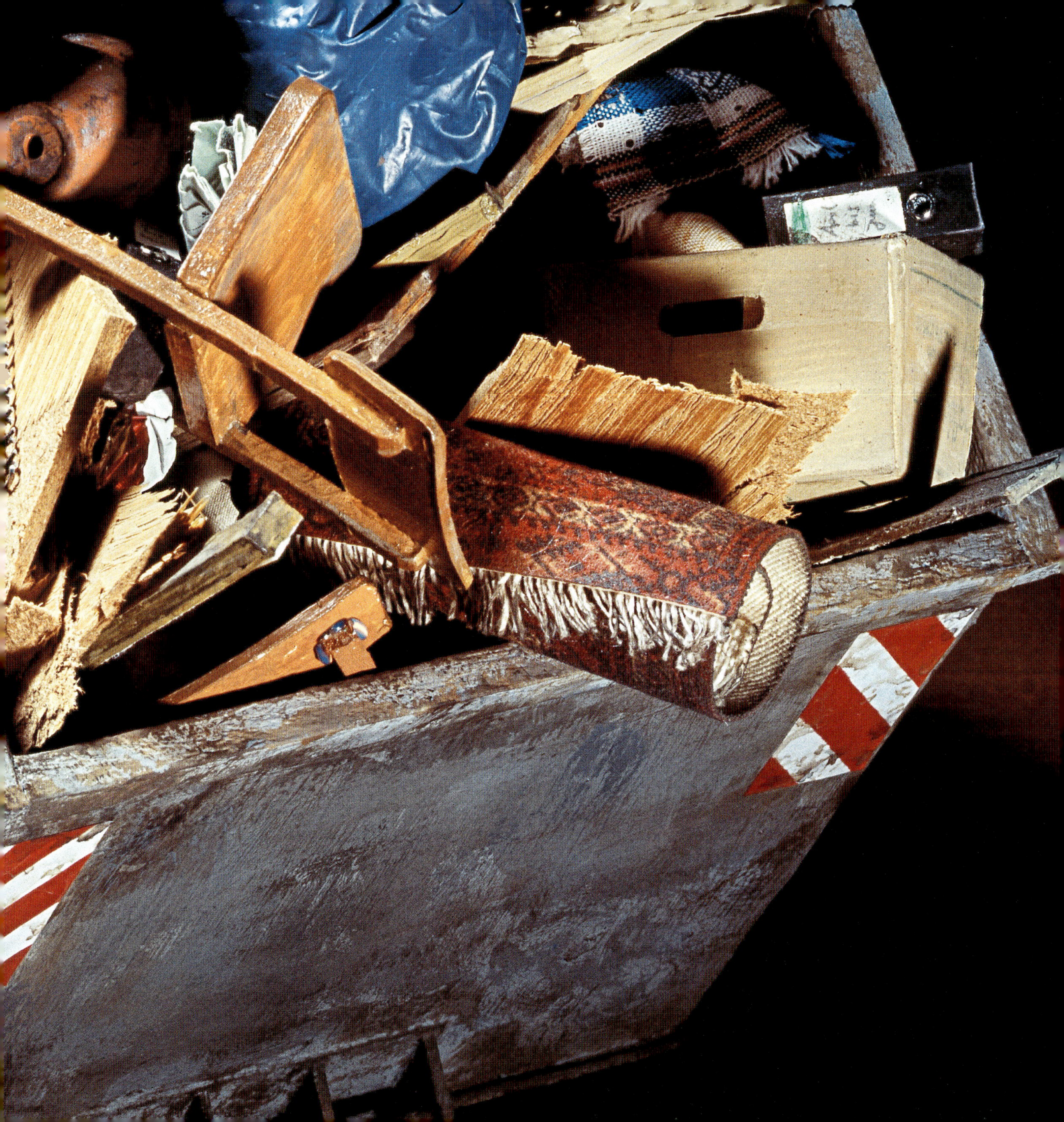

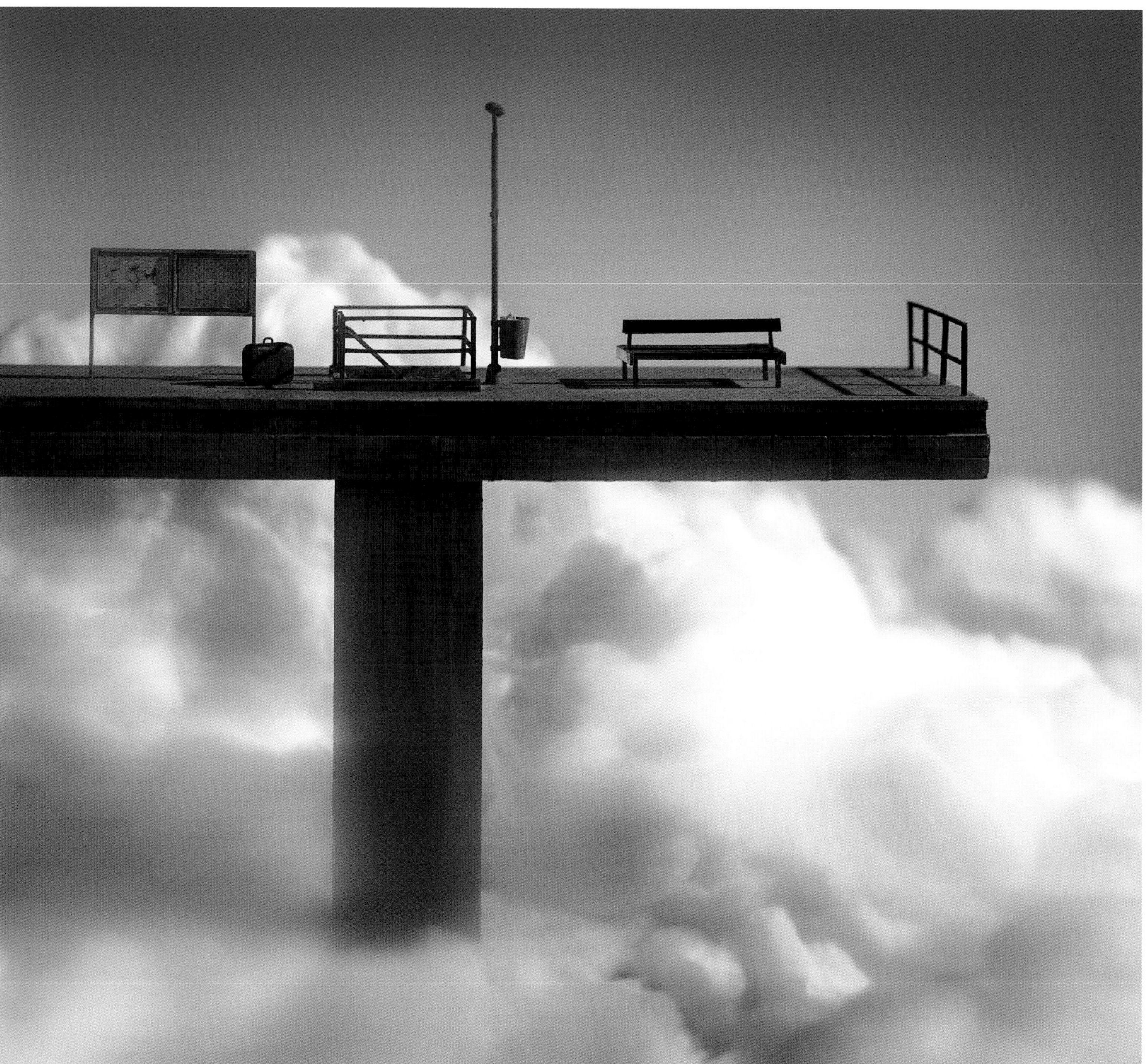

Flugsteig | Departure Gate
2002

Tennis-Halfpipe | Tennis Half-Pipe
2002

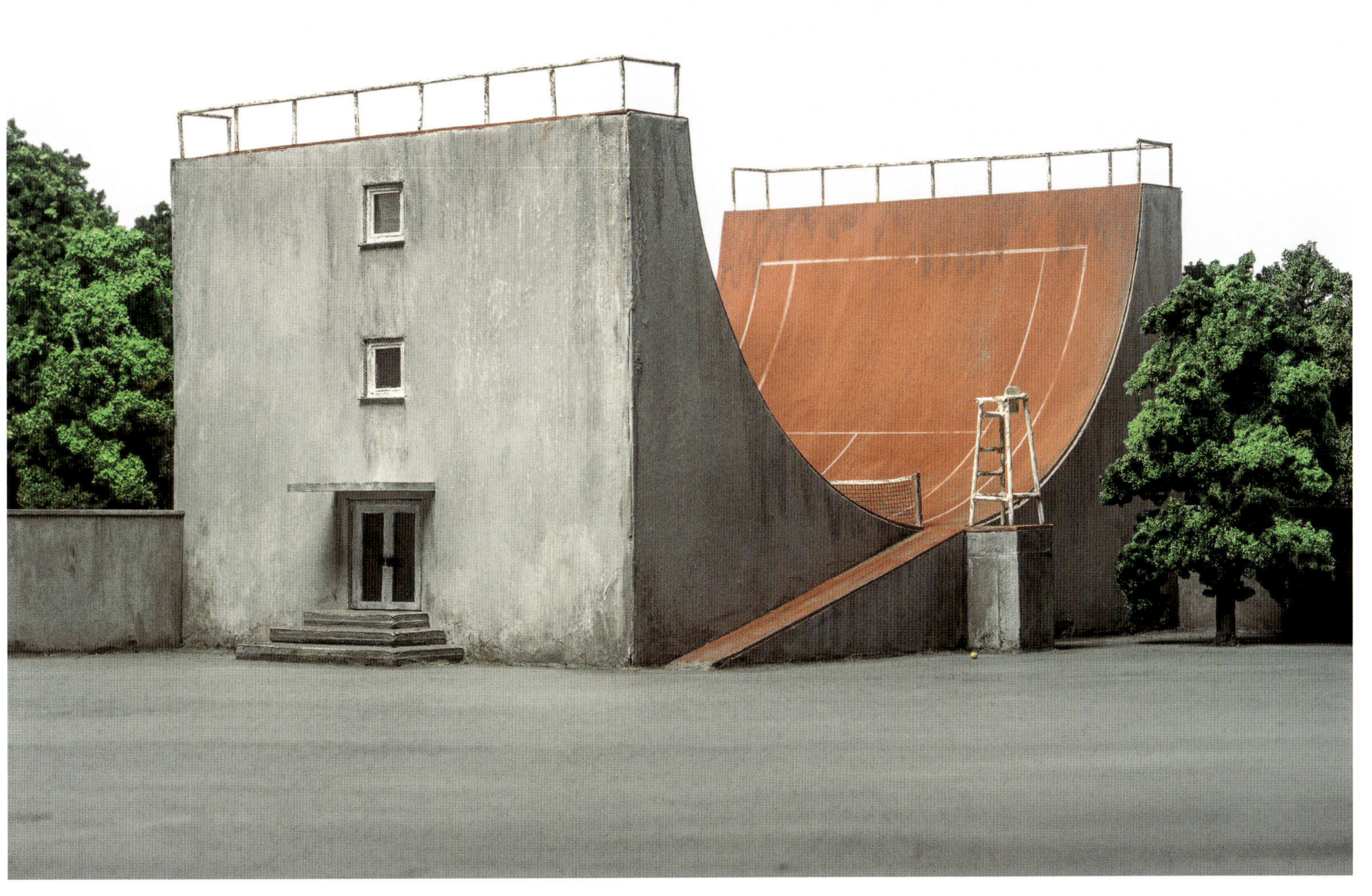

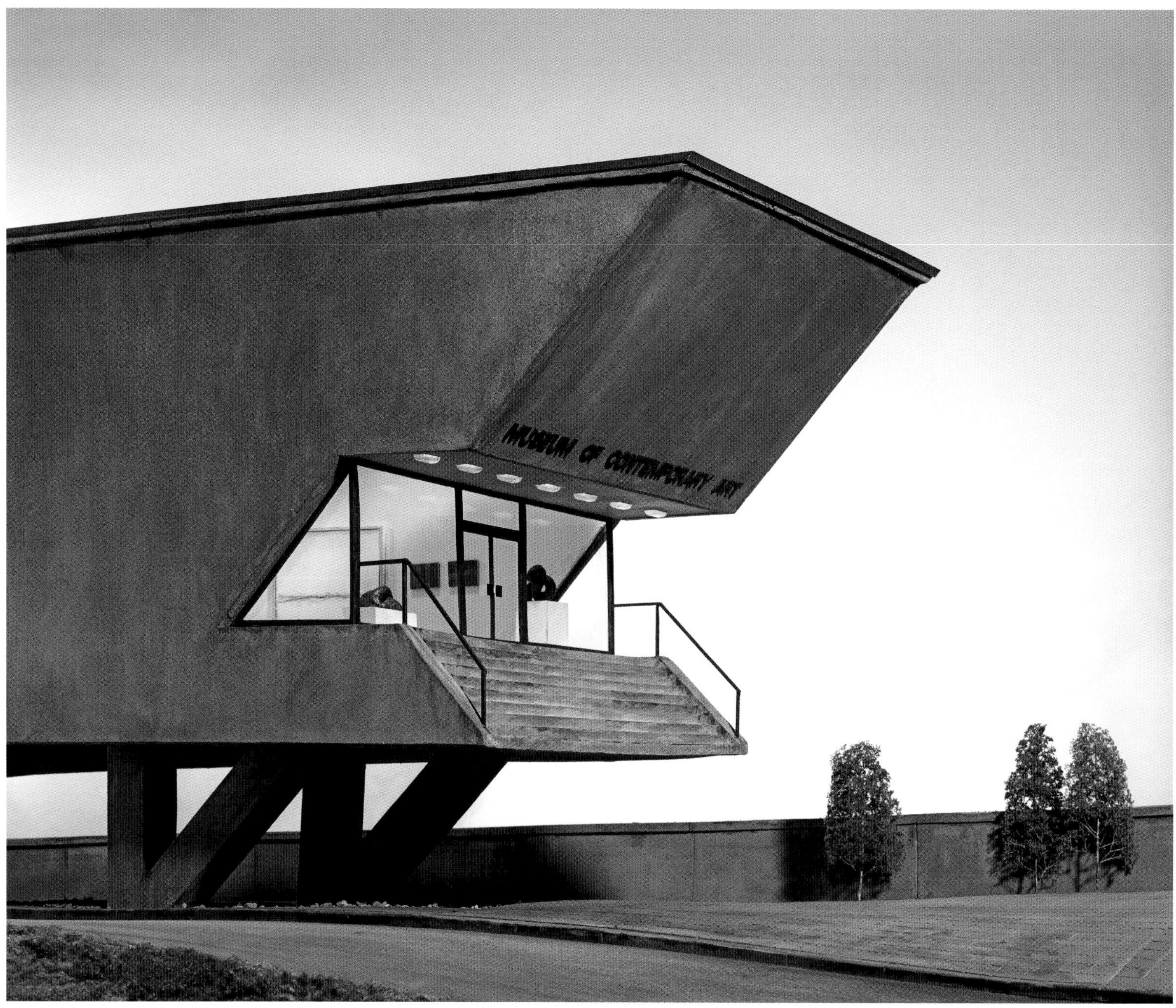
MUSEUM OF CONTEMPORARY ART

Auf hohem Niveau | At a High Level
2008

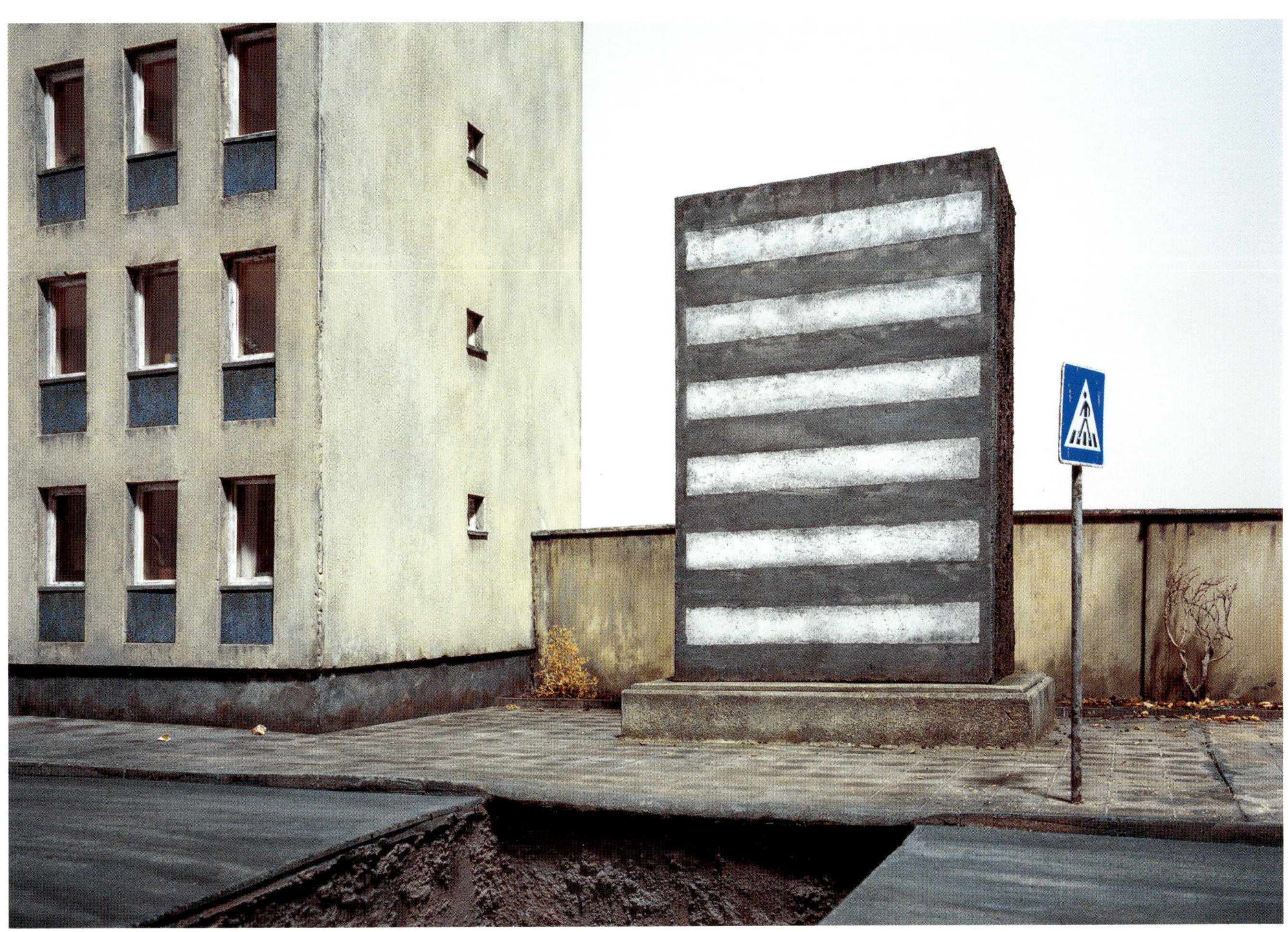

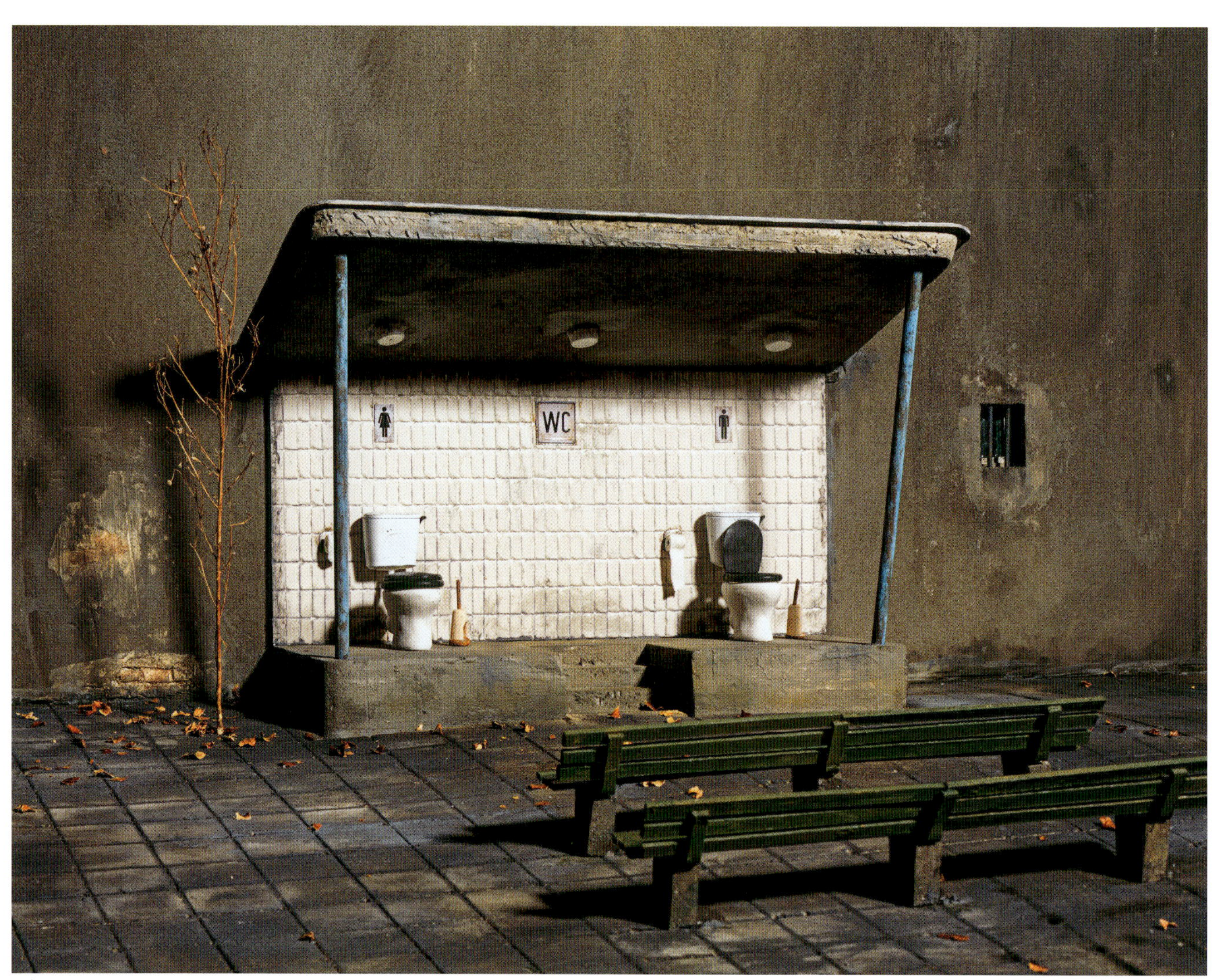
WC

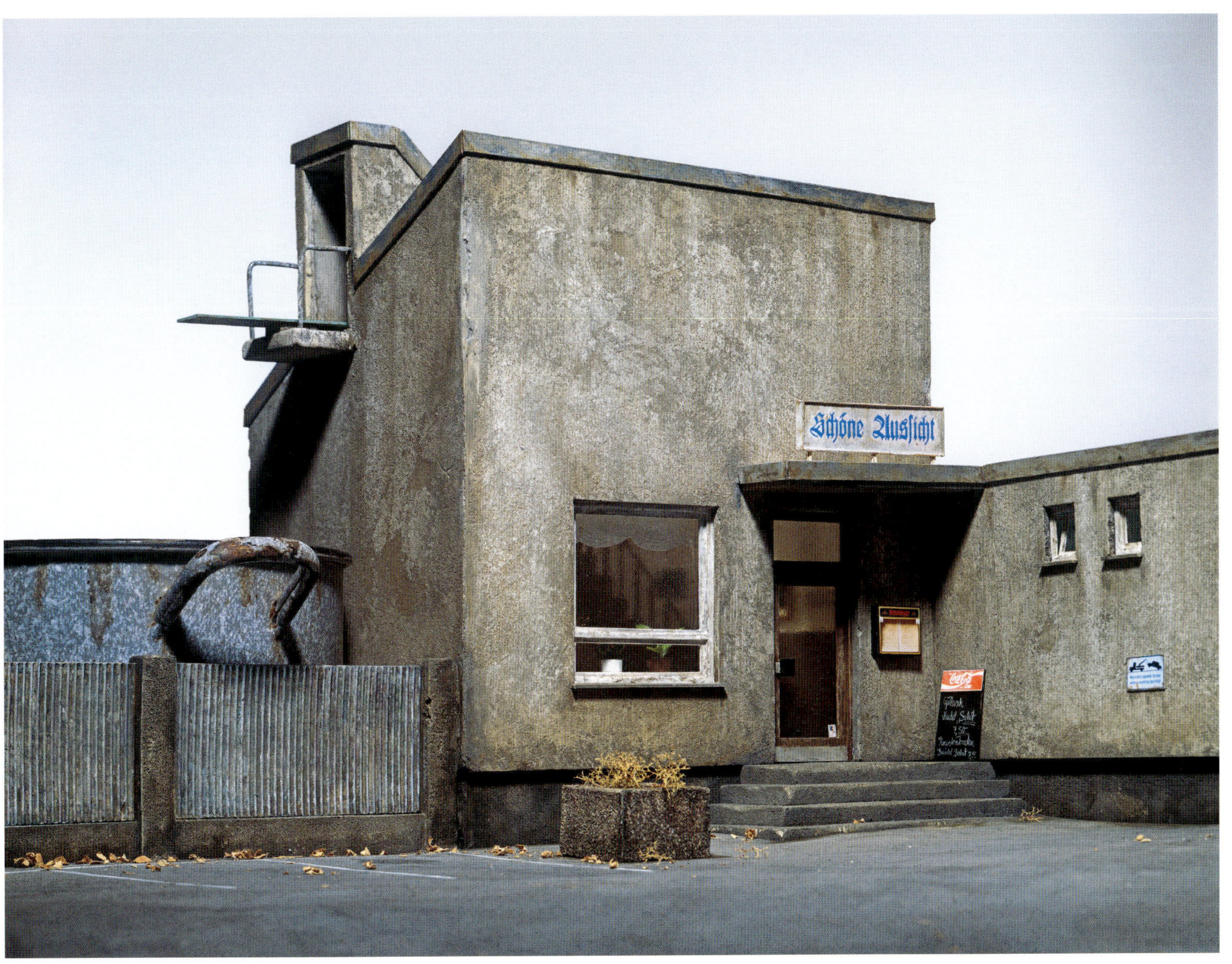
Schöne Aussicht
Coca-Cola

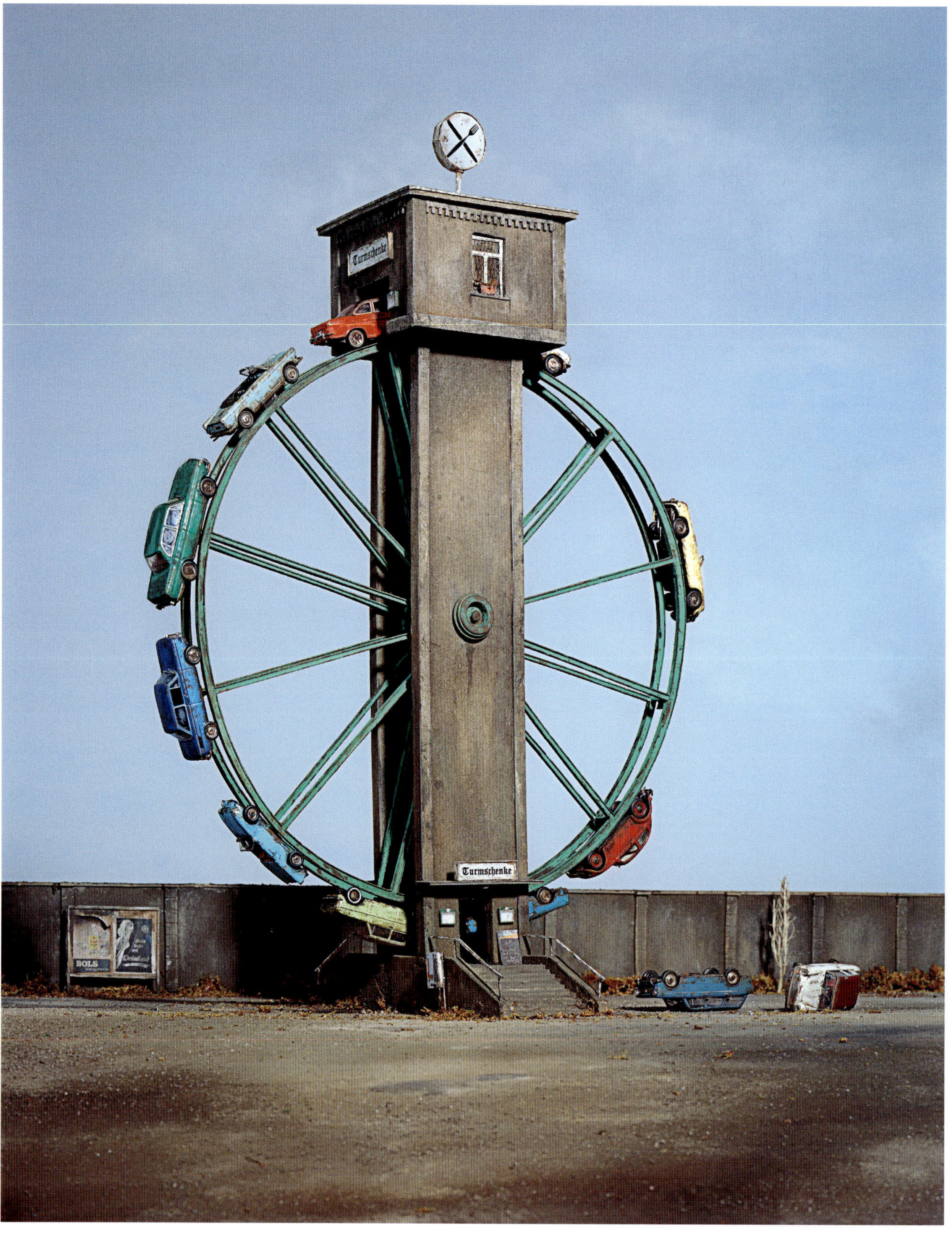
Turmschenke
Turmschenke
BOLS

Drive-In
2012

Golden Goal
2003

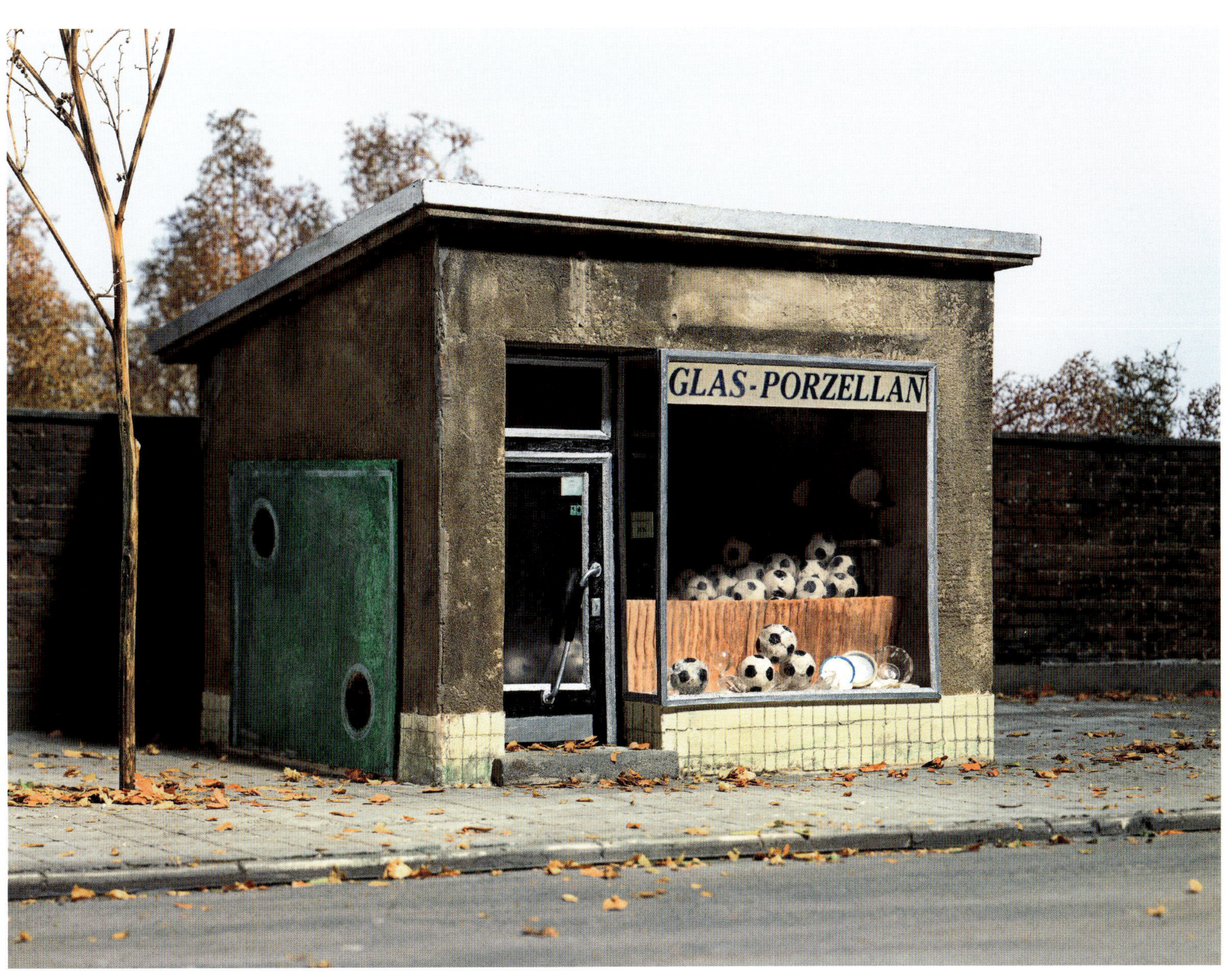
GLAS-PORZELLAN

In Autobahnnähe | Near the Autobahn
2005

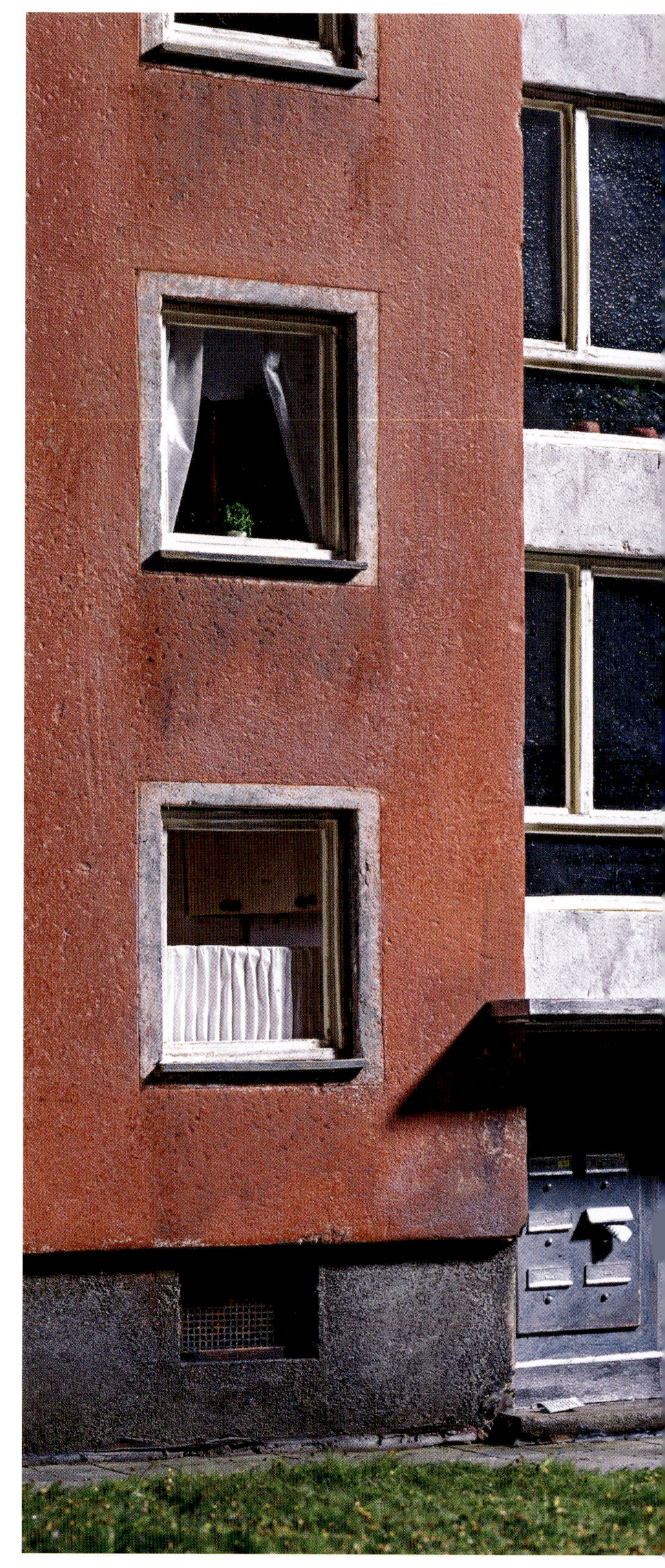

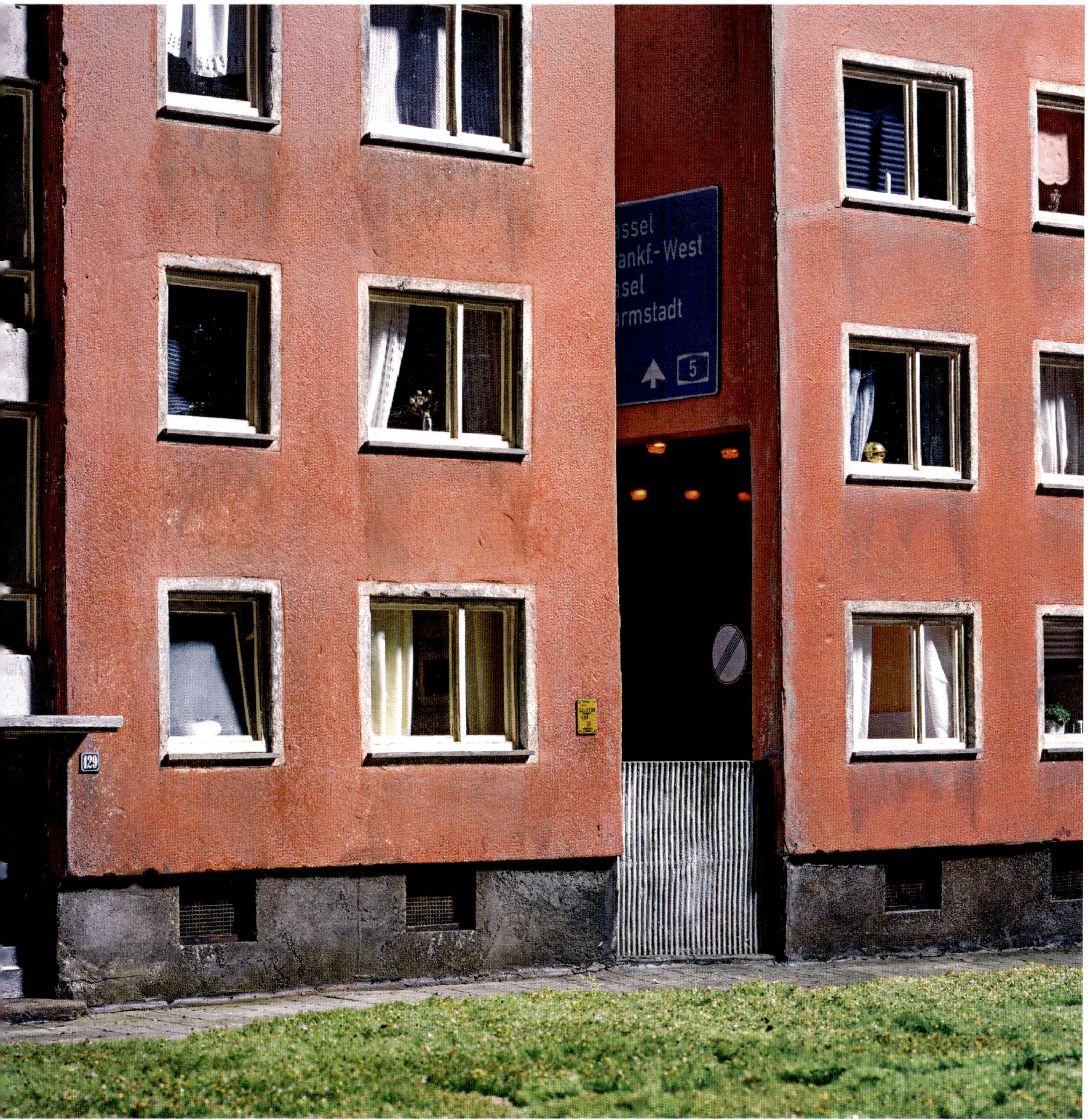
ssel
ankf.-West
sel
rmstadt
5
129

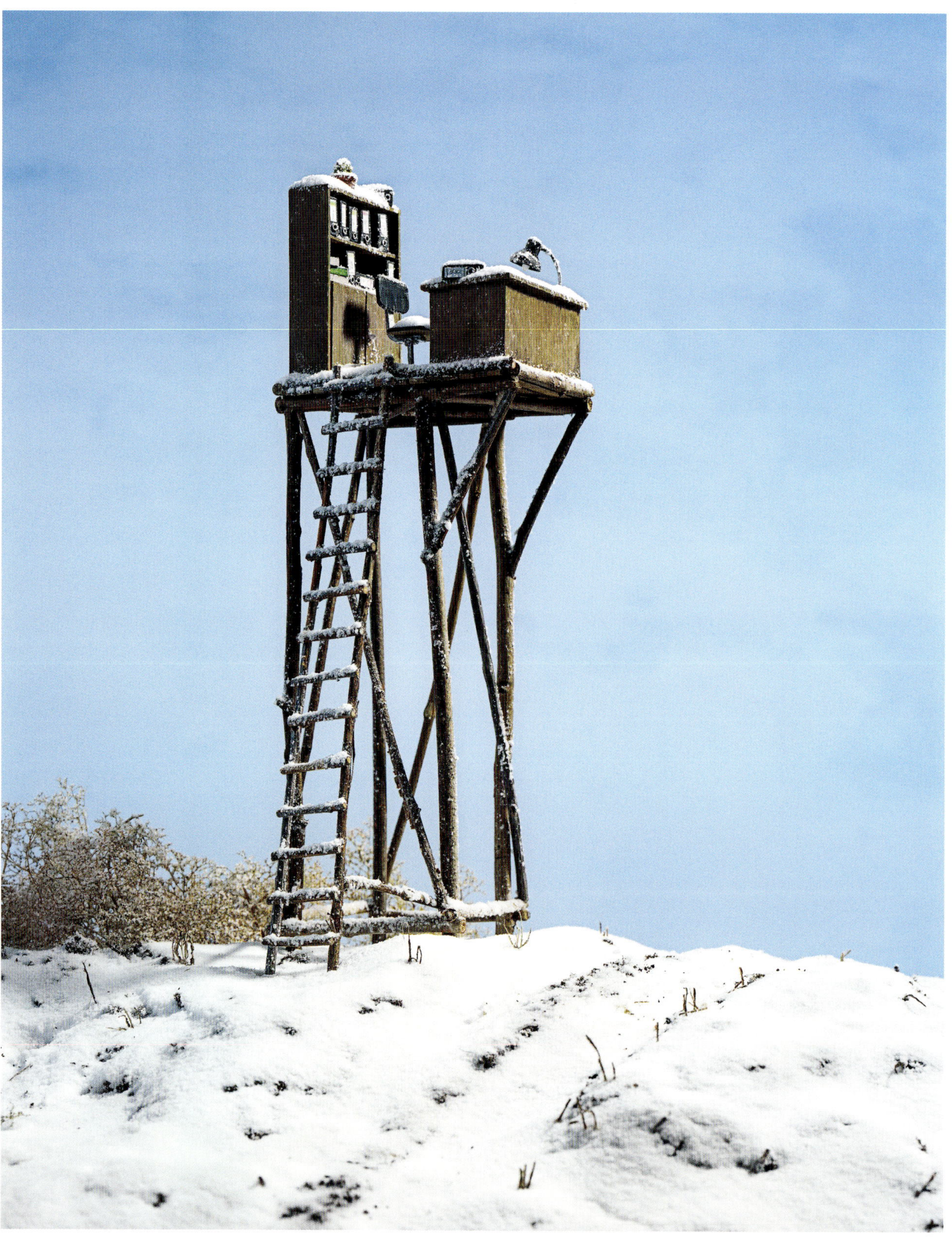

Außendienst | Field Office
2010

Grüne Insel | Green Island
2010

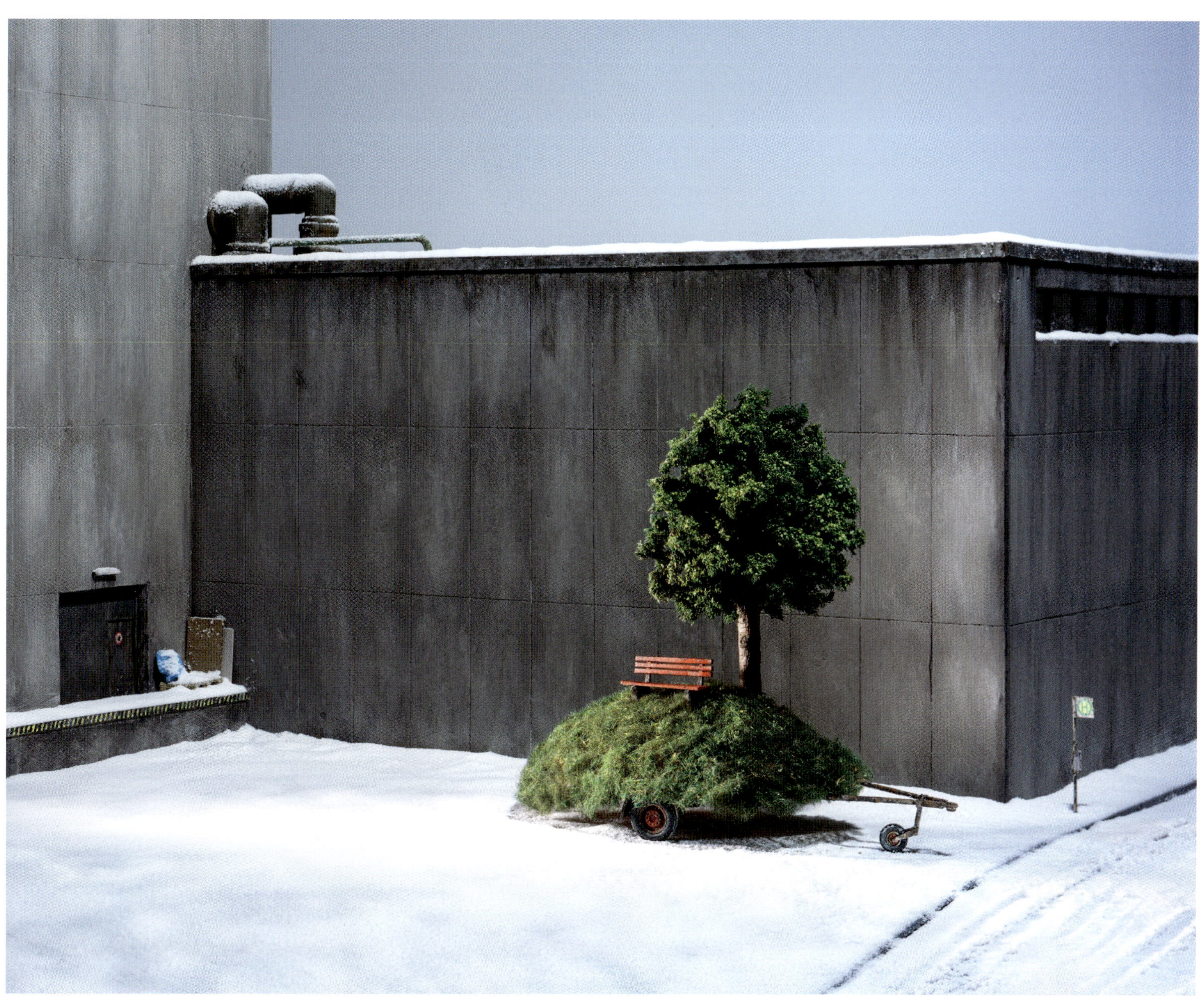

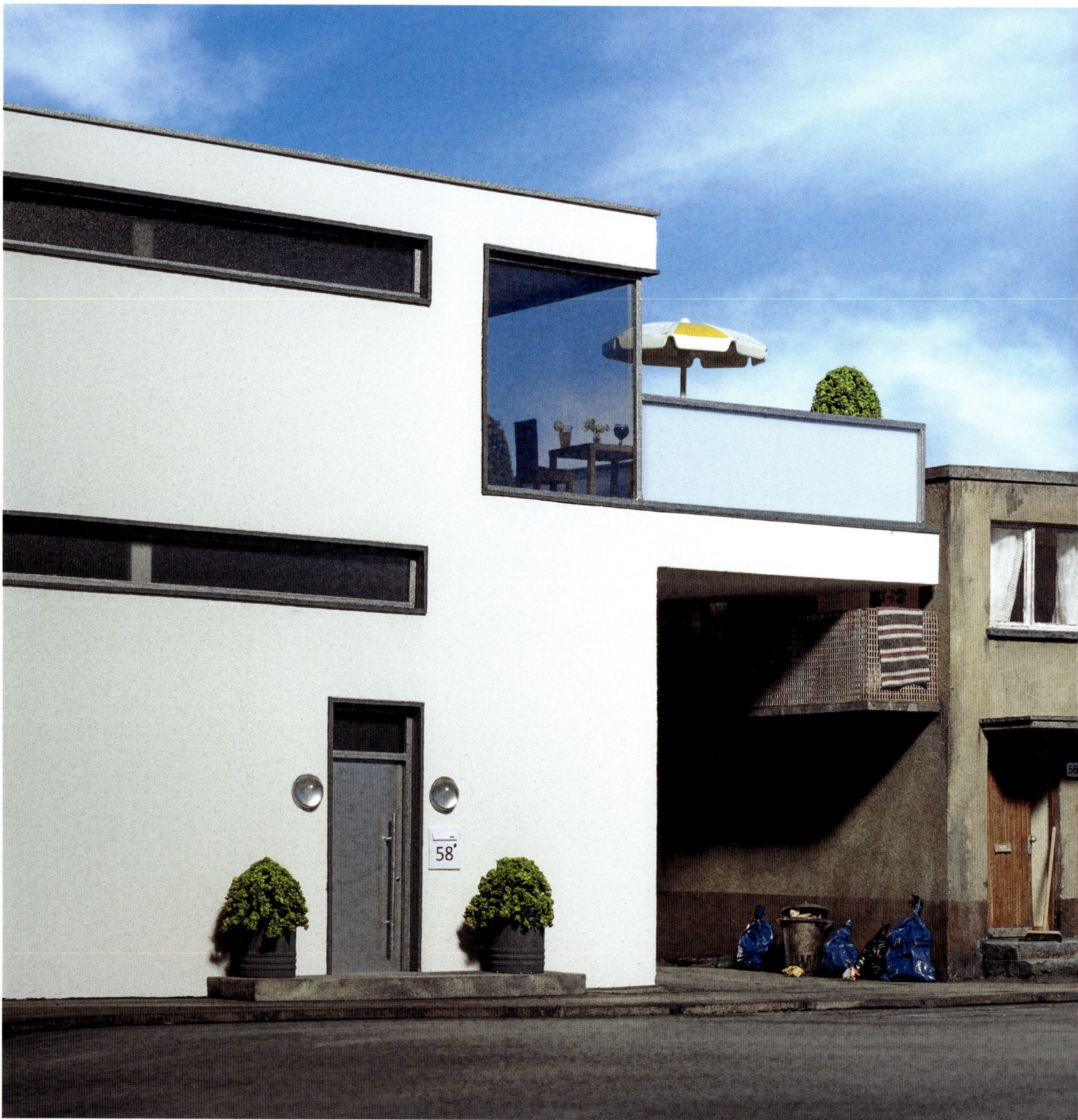
58

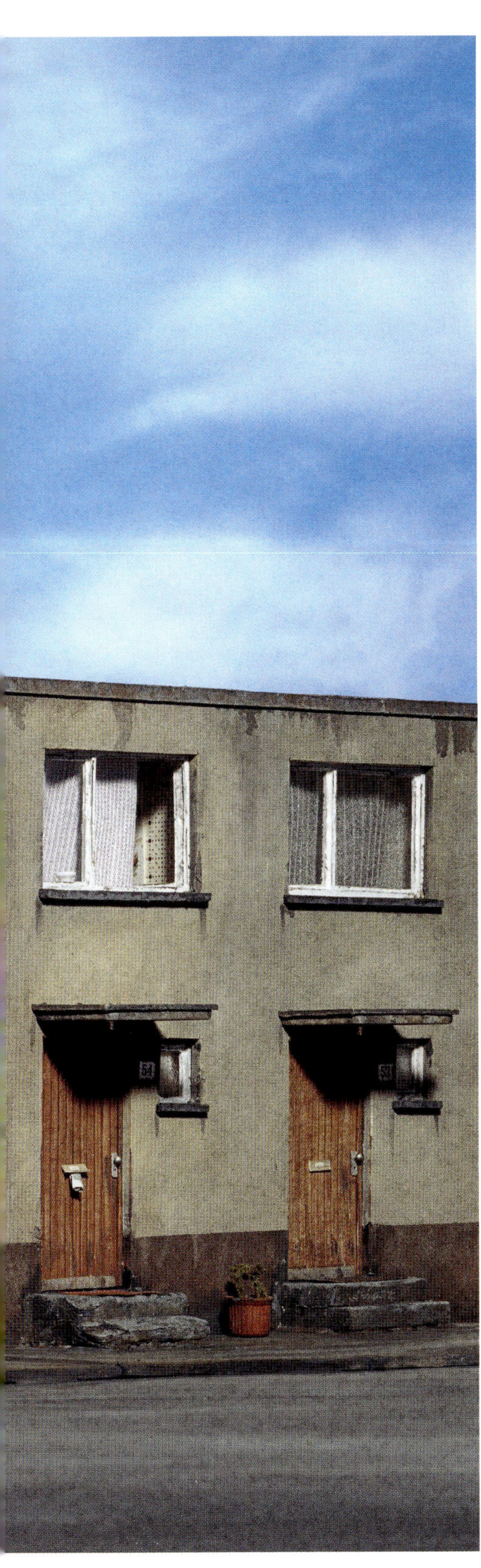

Ein Platz an der Sonne | A Place in the Sun
2014

Kleinod | Small Paradise
2008

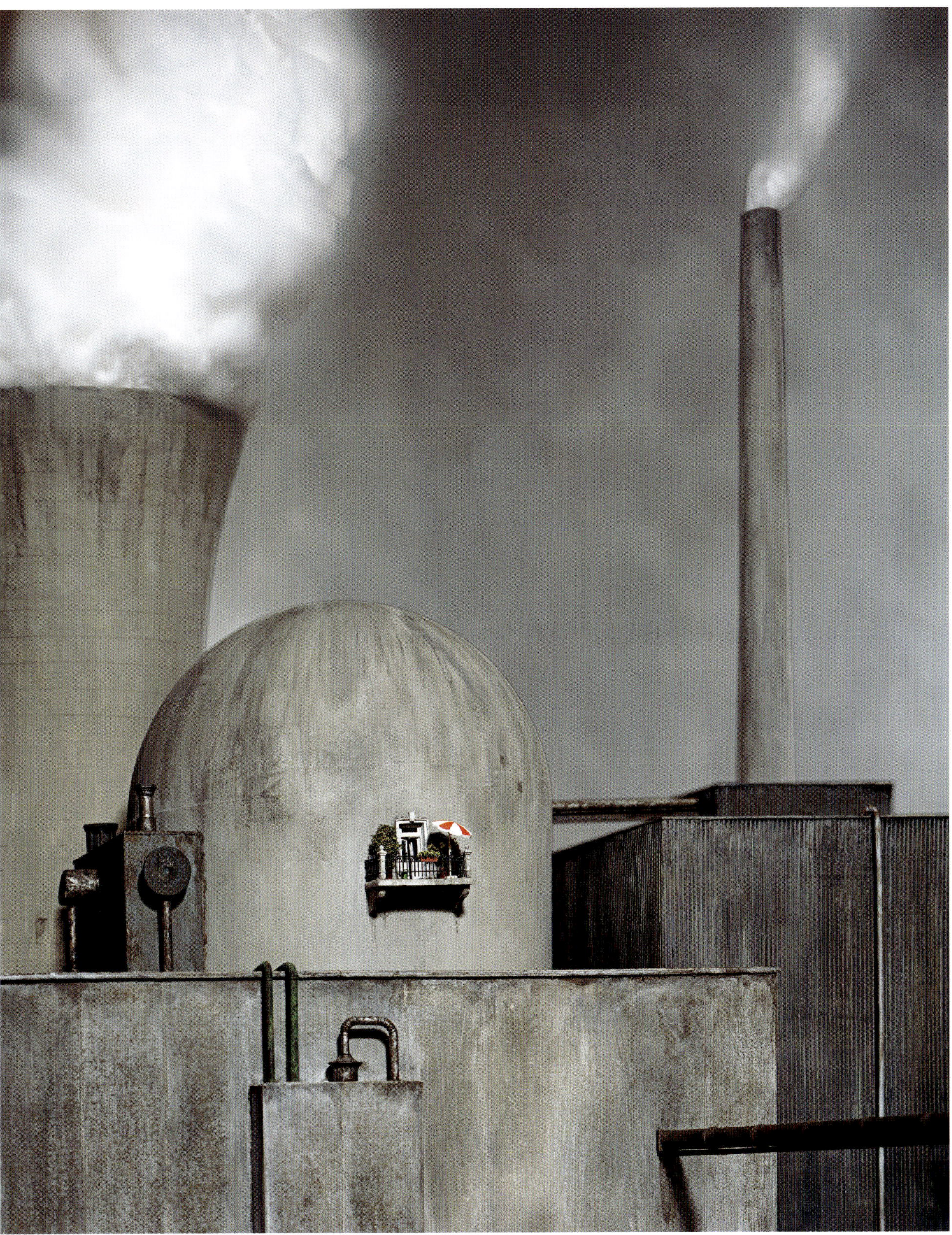

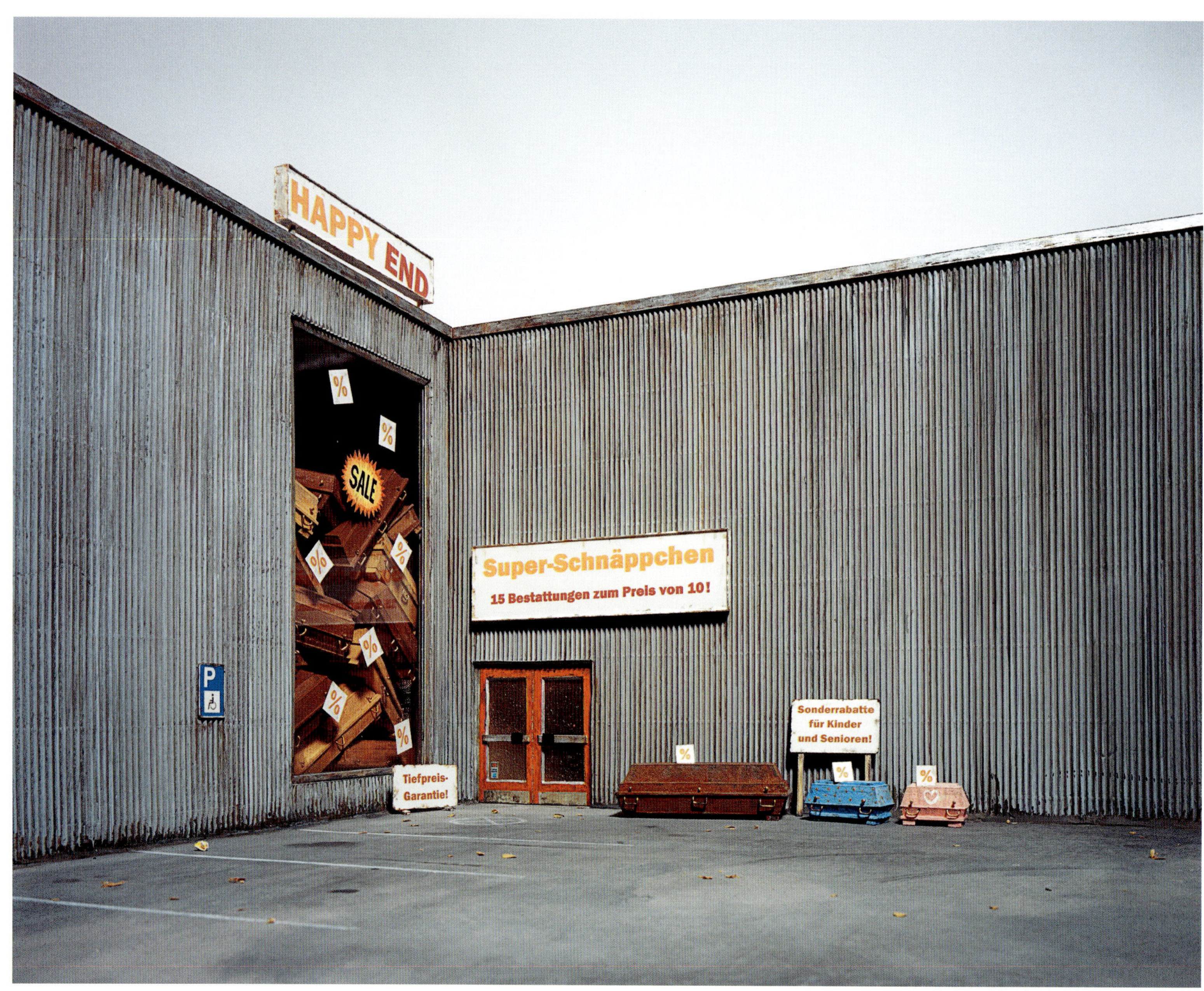
HAPPY END
SALE
Super-Schnäppchen
15 Bestattungen zum Preis von 10!
Tiefpreis-
Garantie!
Sonderrabatte
für Kinder
und Senioren!

Bestattungsdiscounter | Funeral Discounter
2014

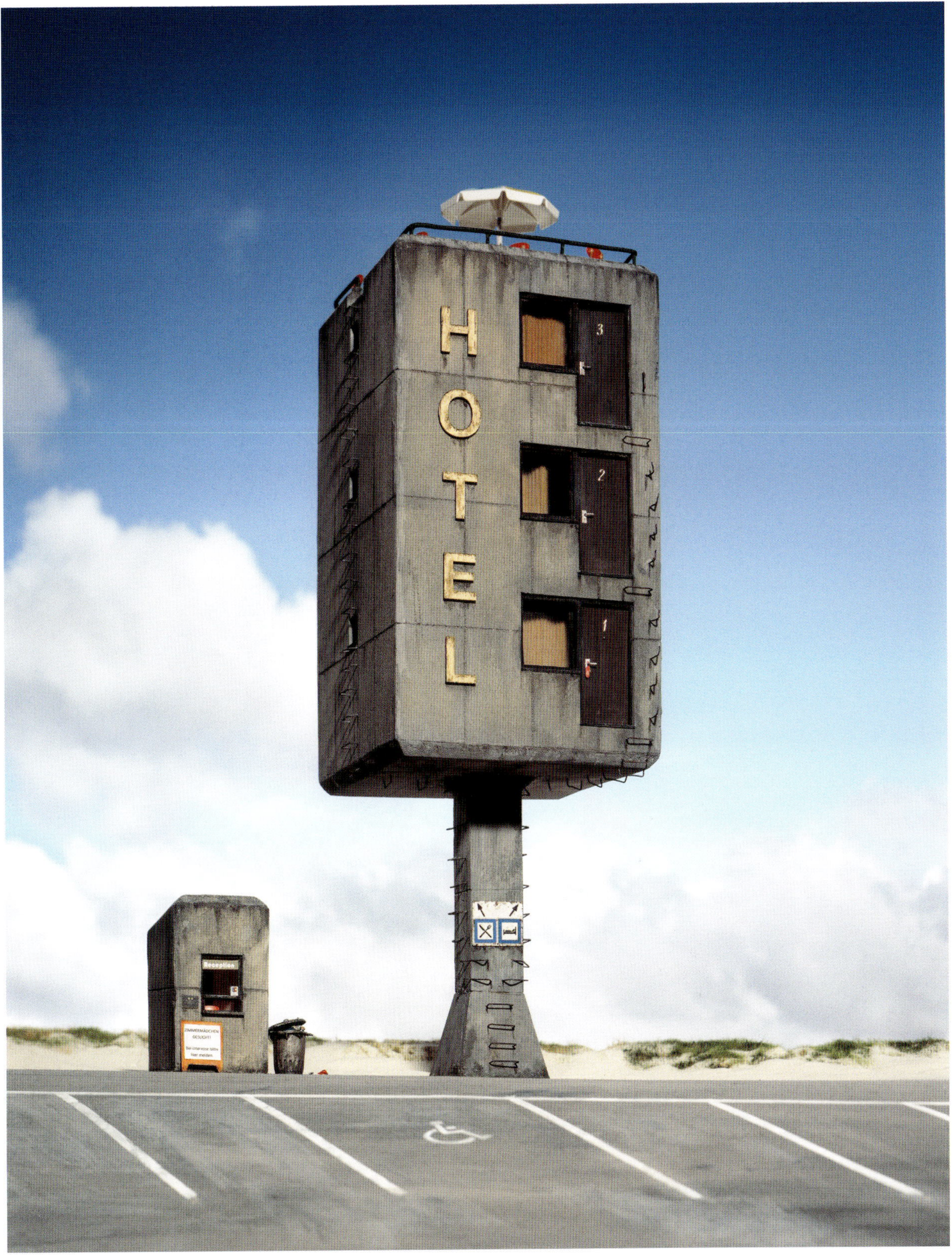
HOTEL
3
2
1
Reception
ZIMMERMÄDCHEN
GESUCHT!

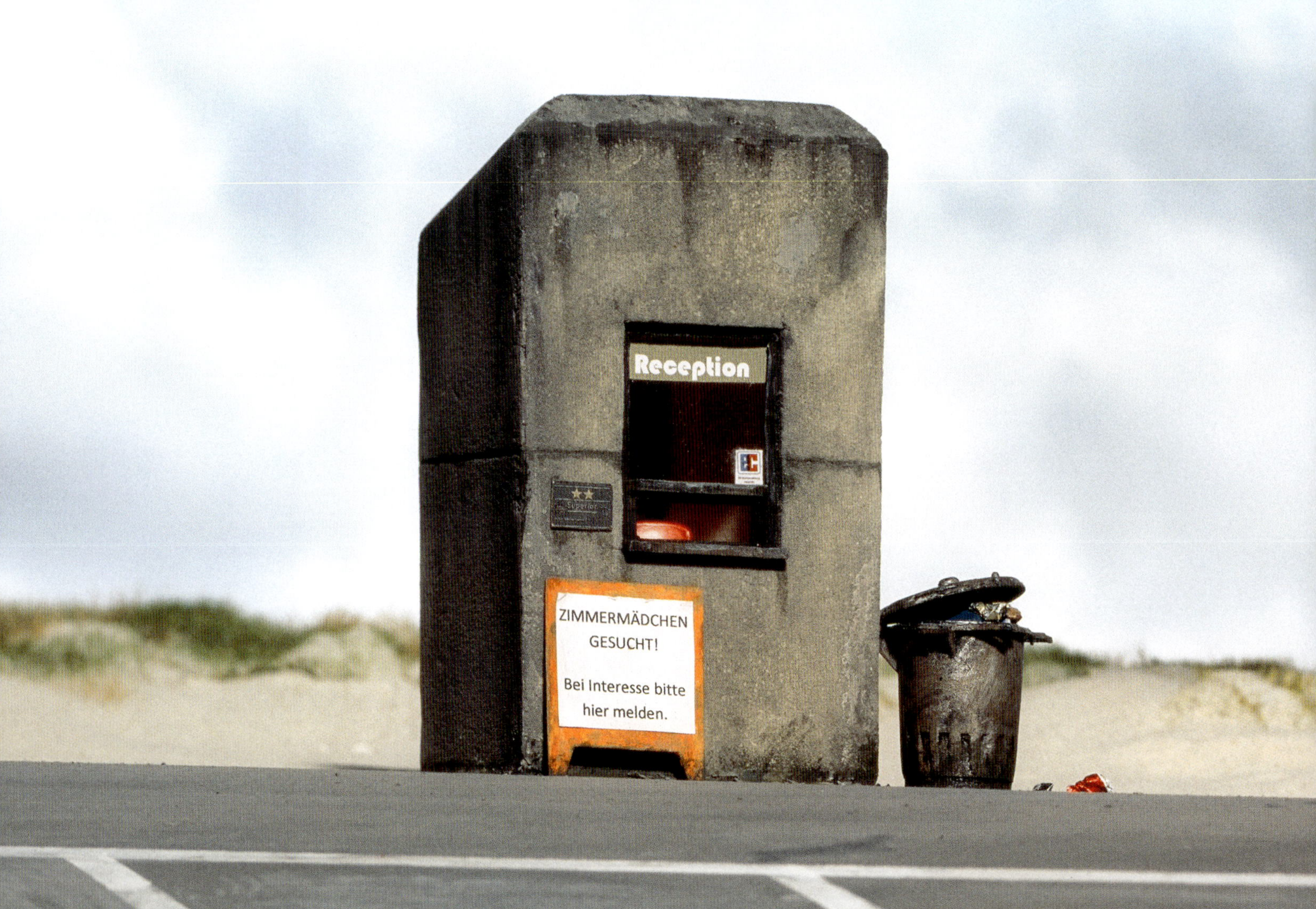
Reception
ZIMMERMÄDCHEN
GESUCHT!
Bei Interesse bitte
hier melden.

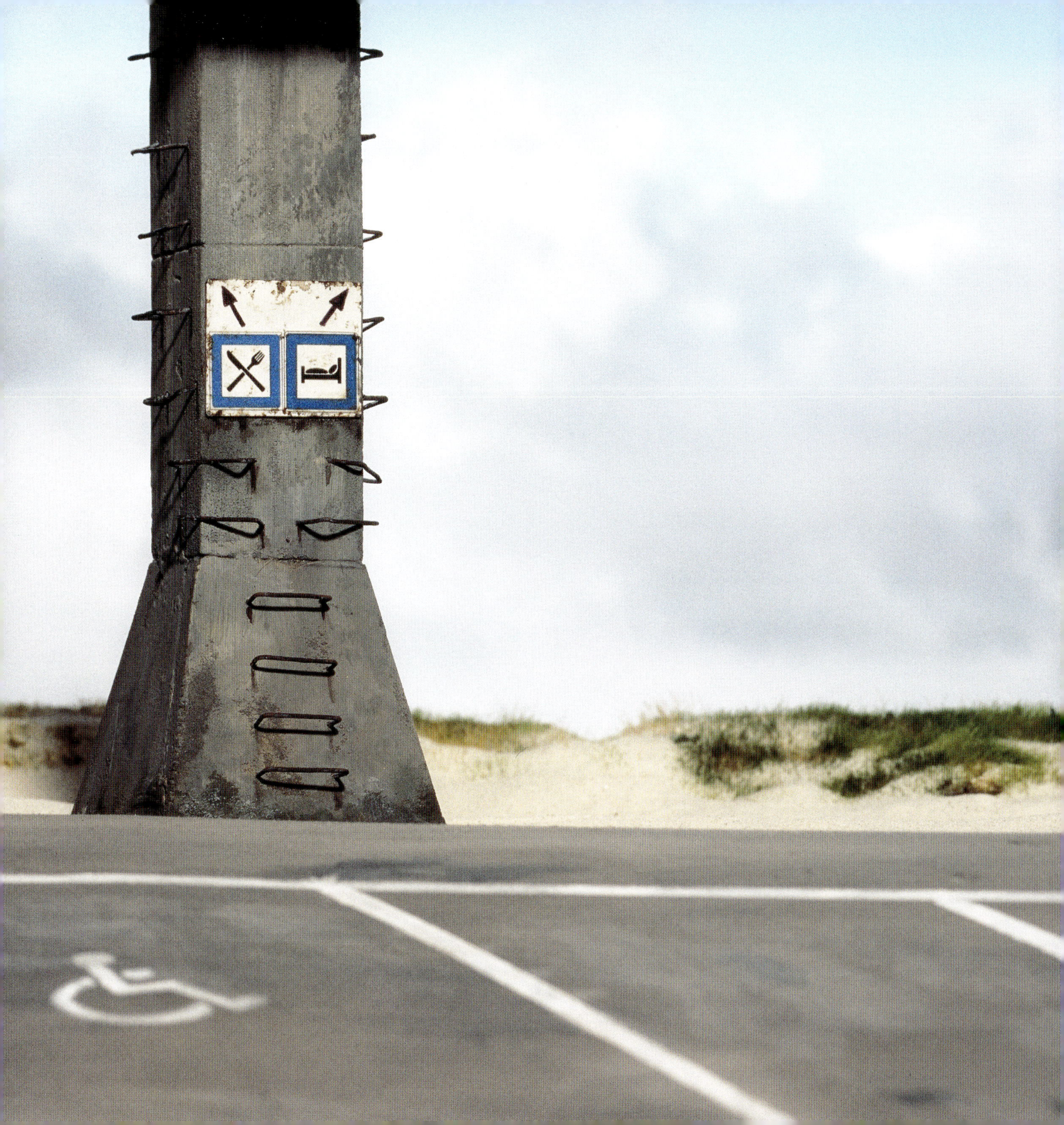

Himmelspforte | Heaven's Gate
2010

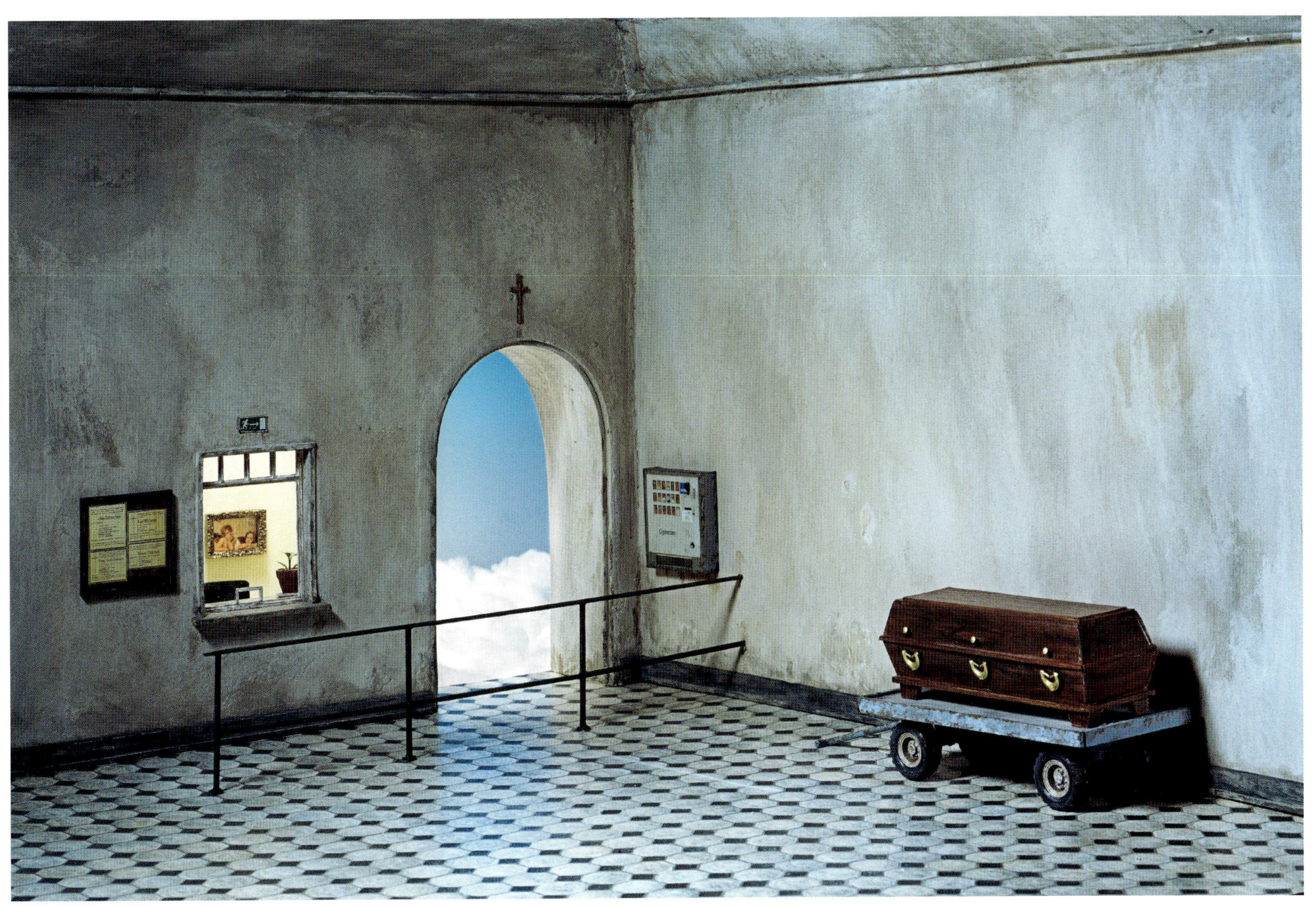

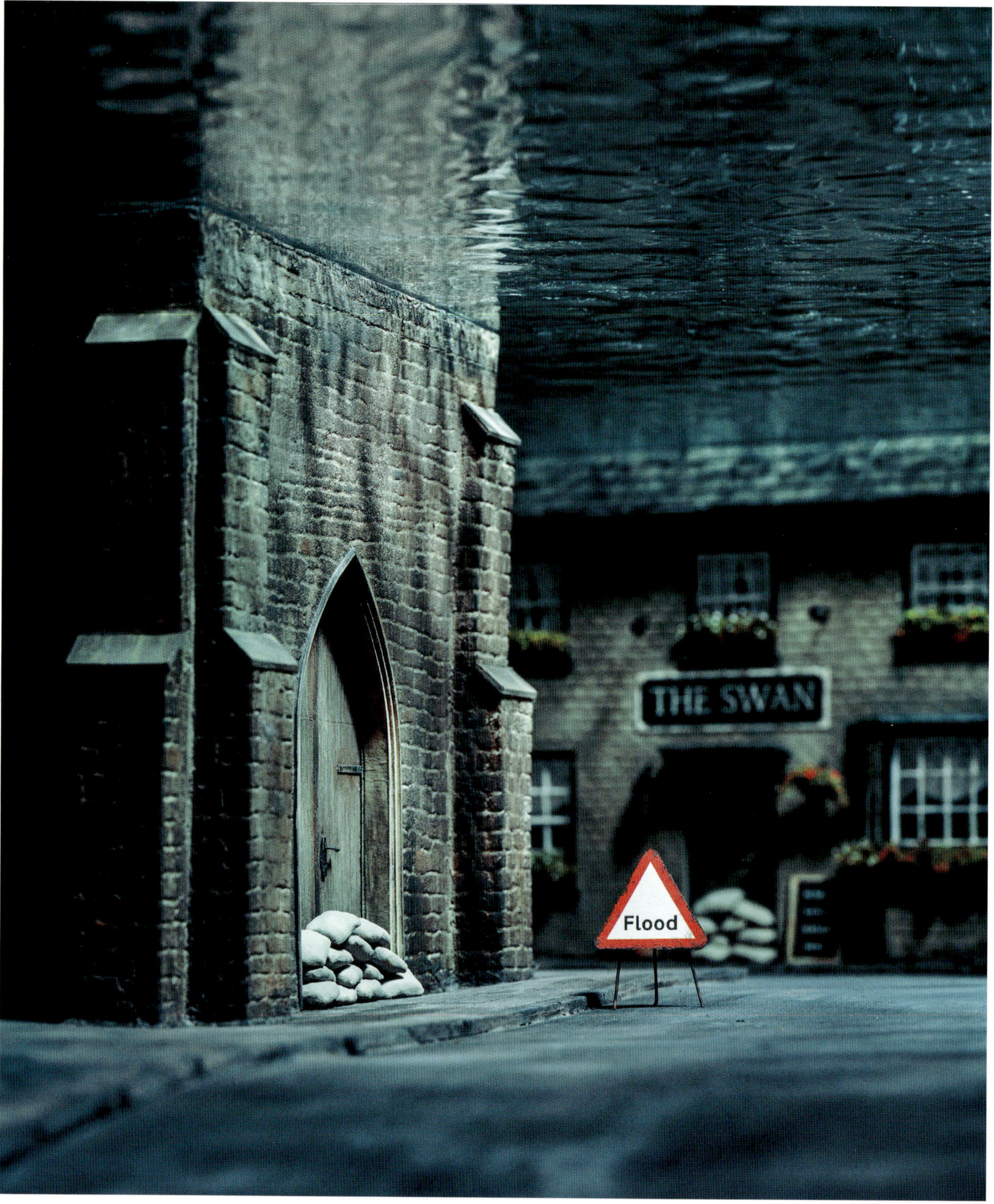
THE SWAN
Flood

Flood
2015

Erlösung | Salvation
2009

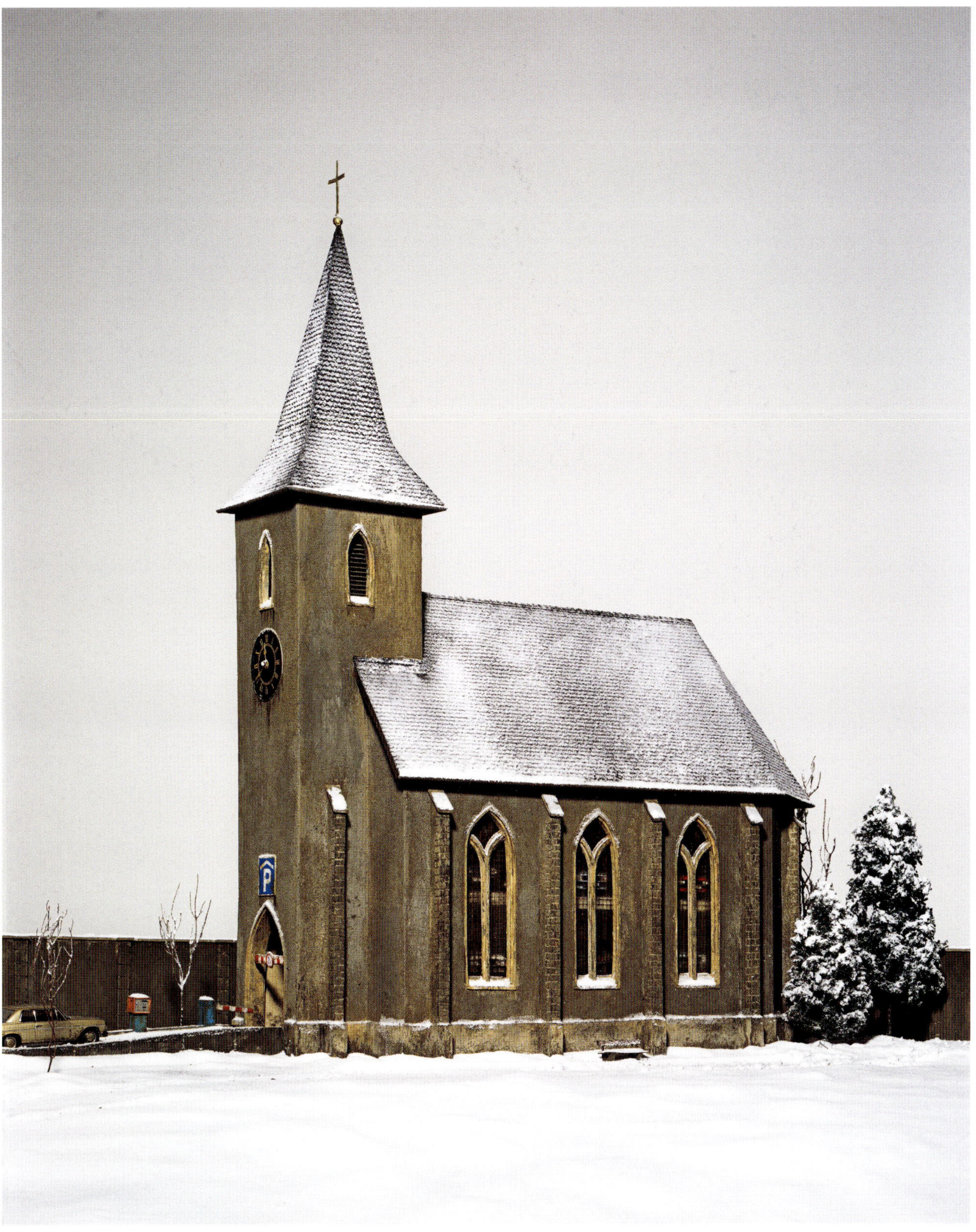

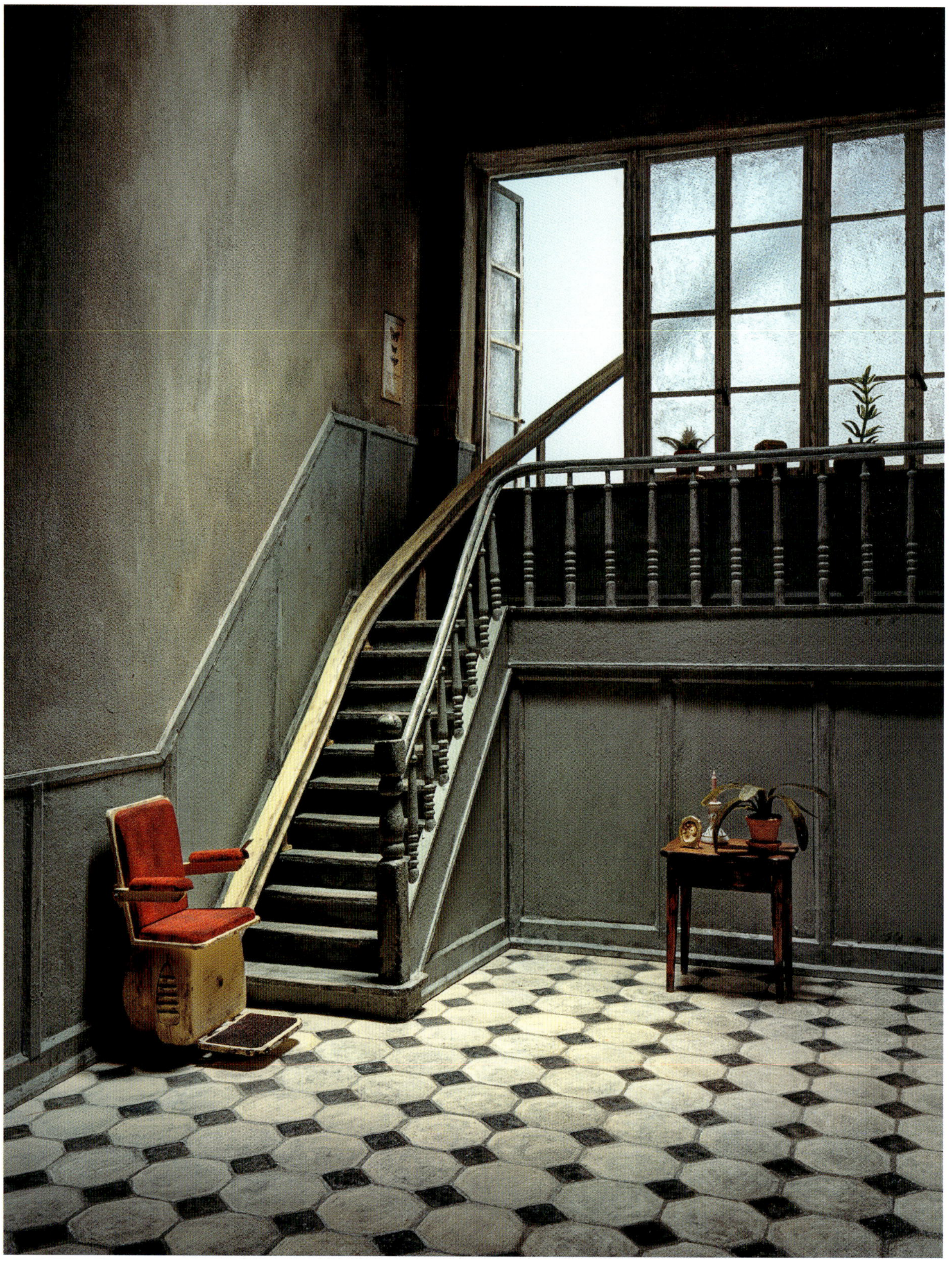

Hoch hinaus | Flying High
2016

Das Leben geht weiter | Life Goes On
2003

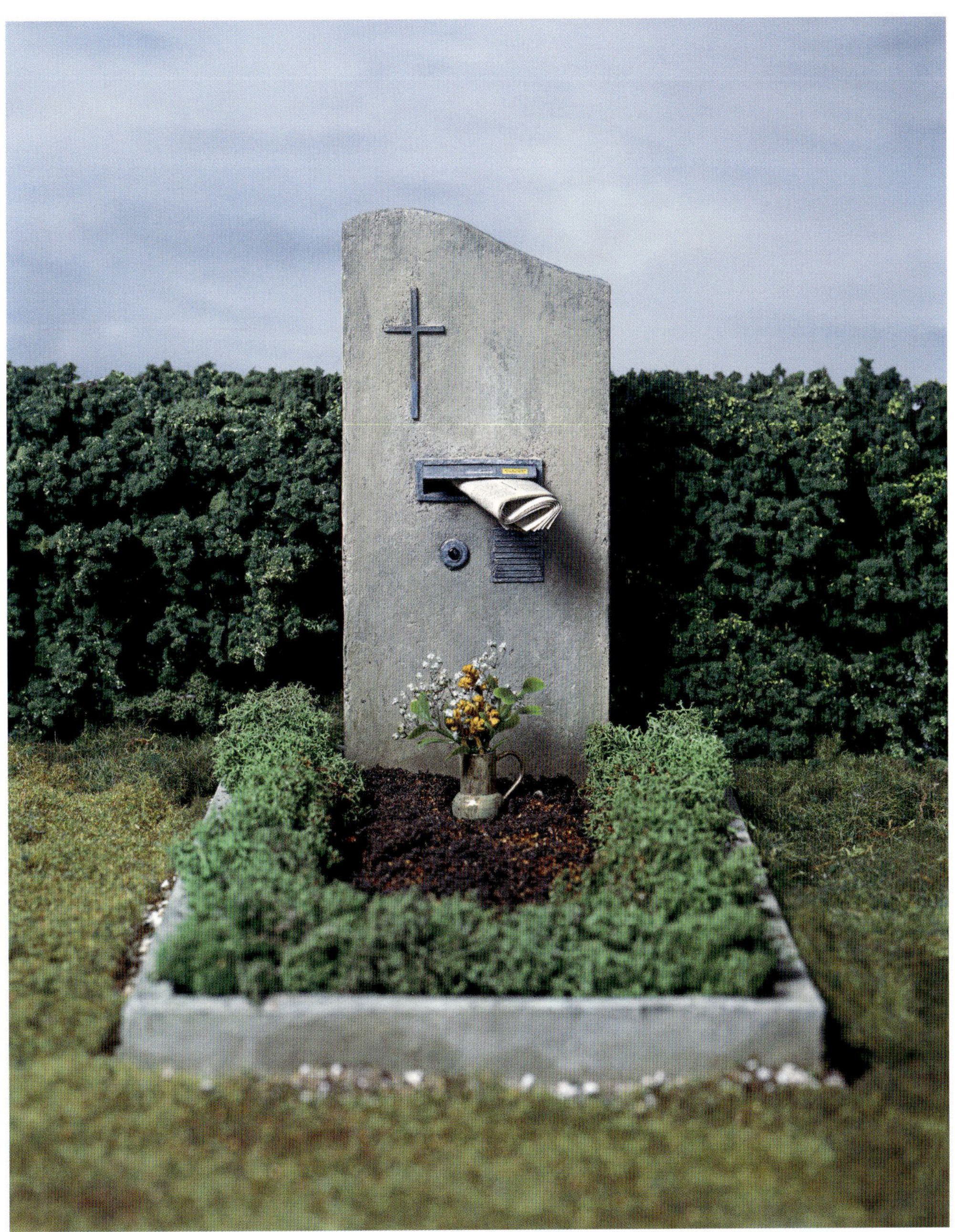

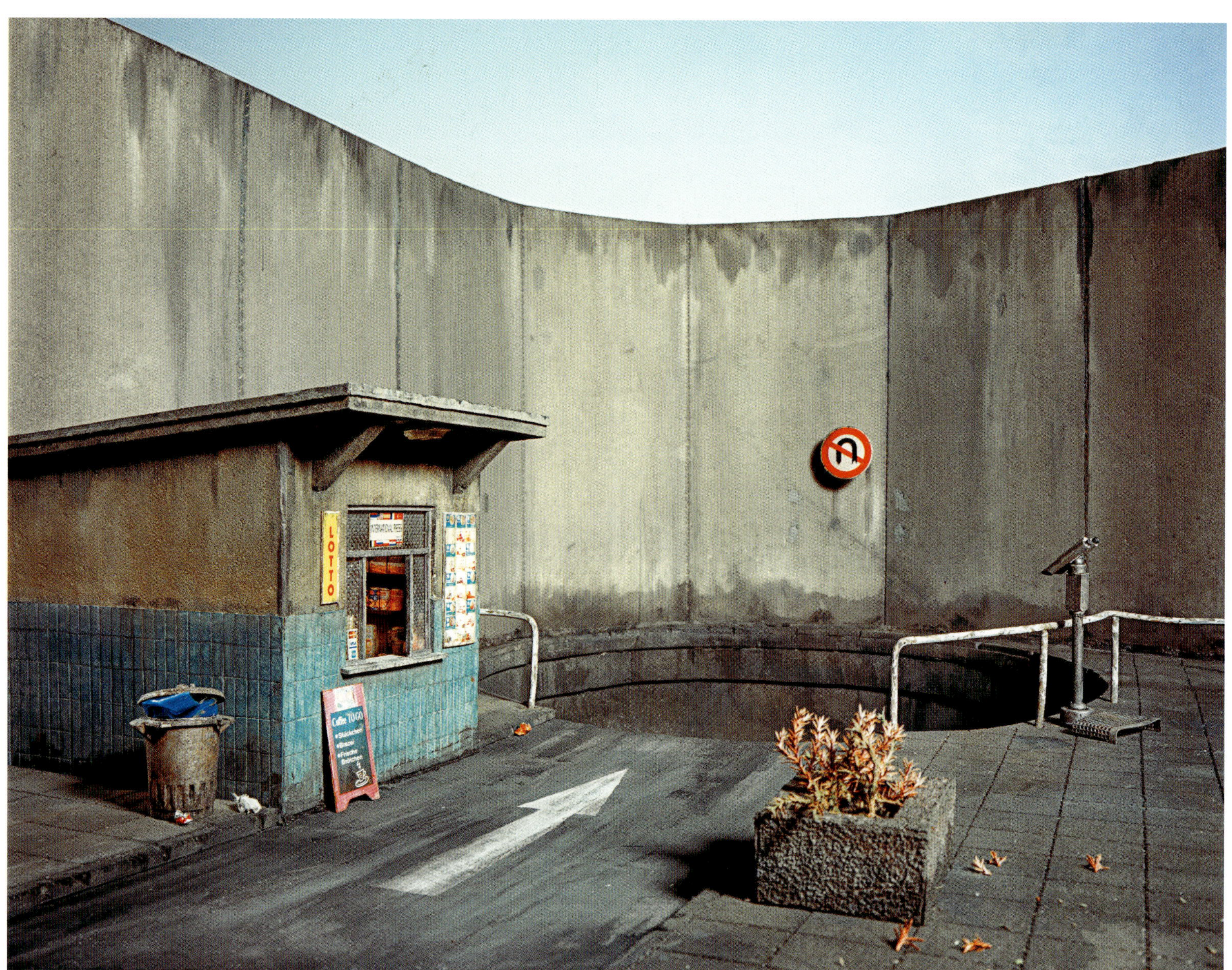

LOTTO
INTERNATIONAL PRESS
Coffee TO GO
Stückchen
Brezel
Frische Brötchen

Abwärts | Downward
2013

Ewige Liebe | Eternal Love
2014

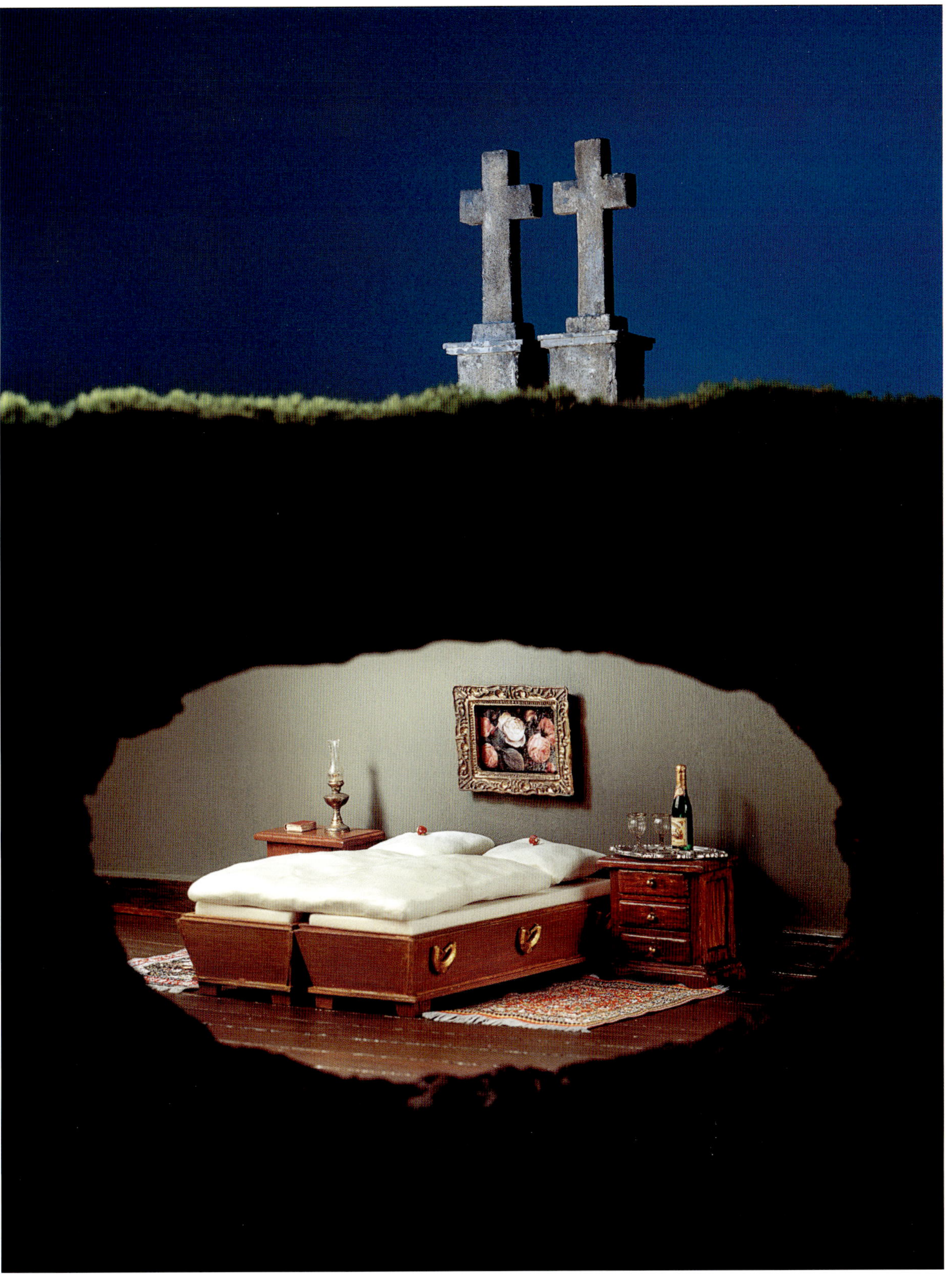

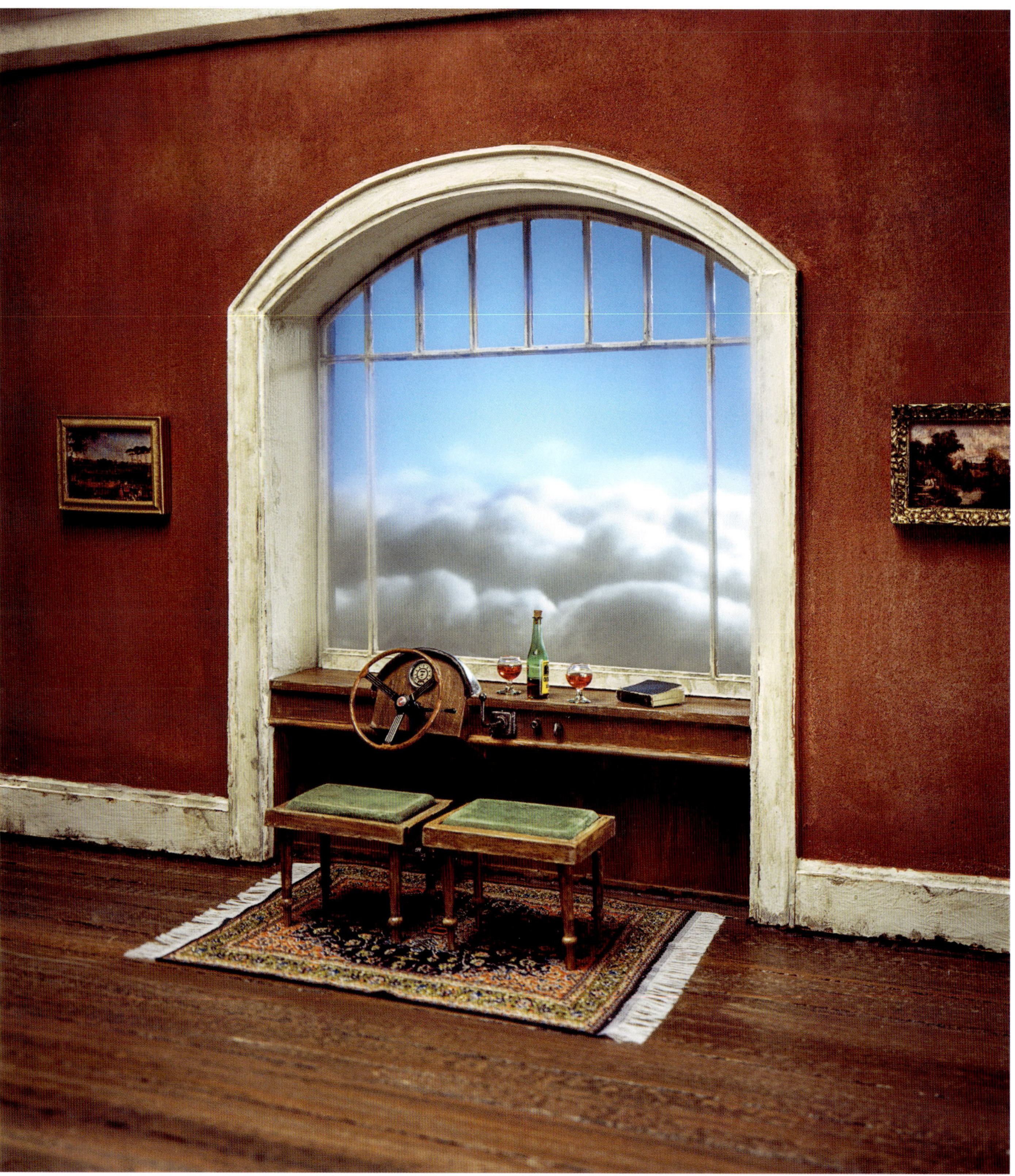

Traumreise | A Dream Trip
2016

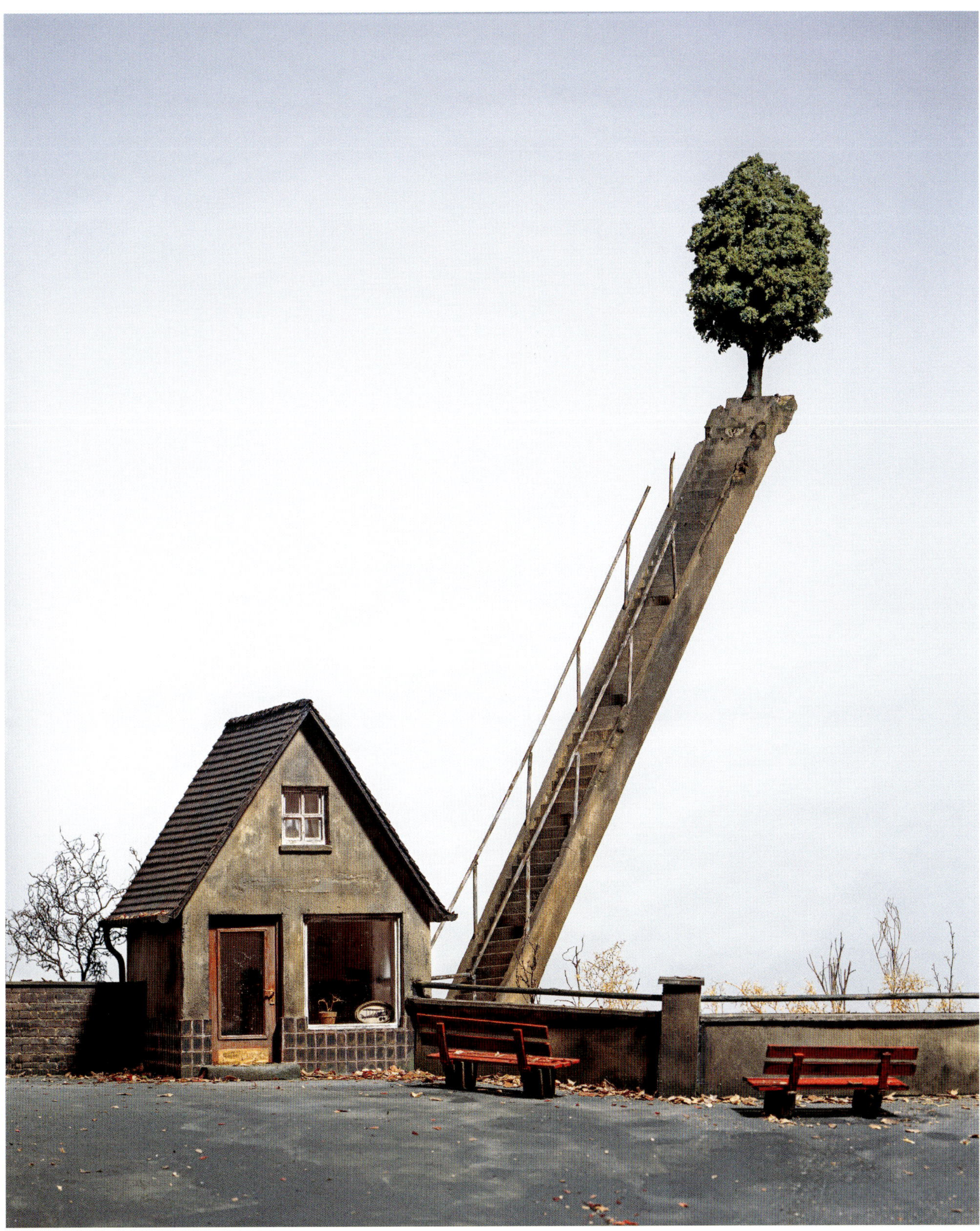

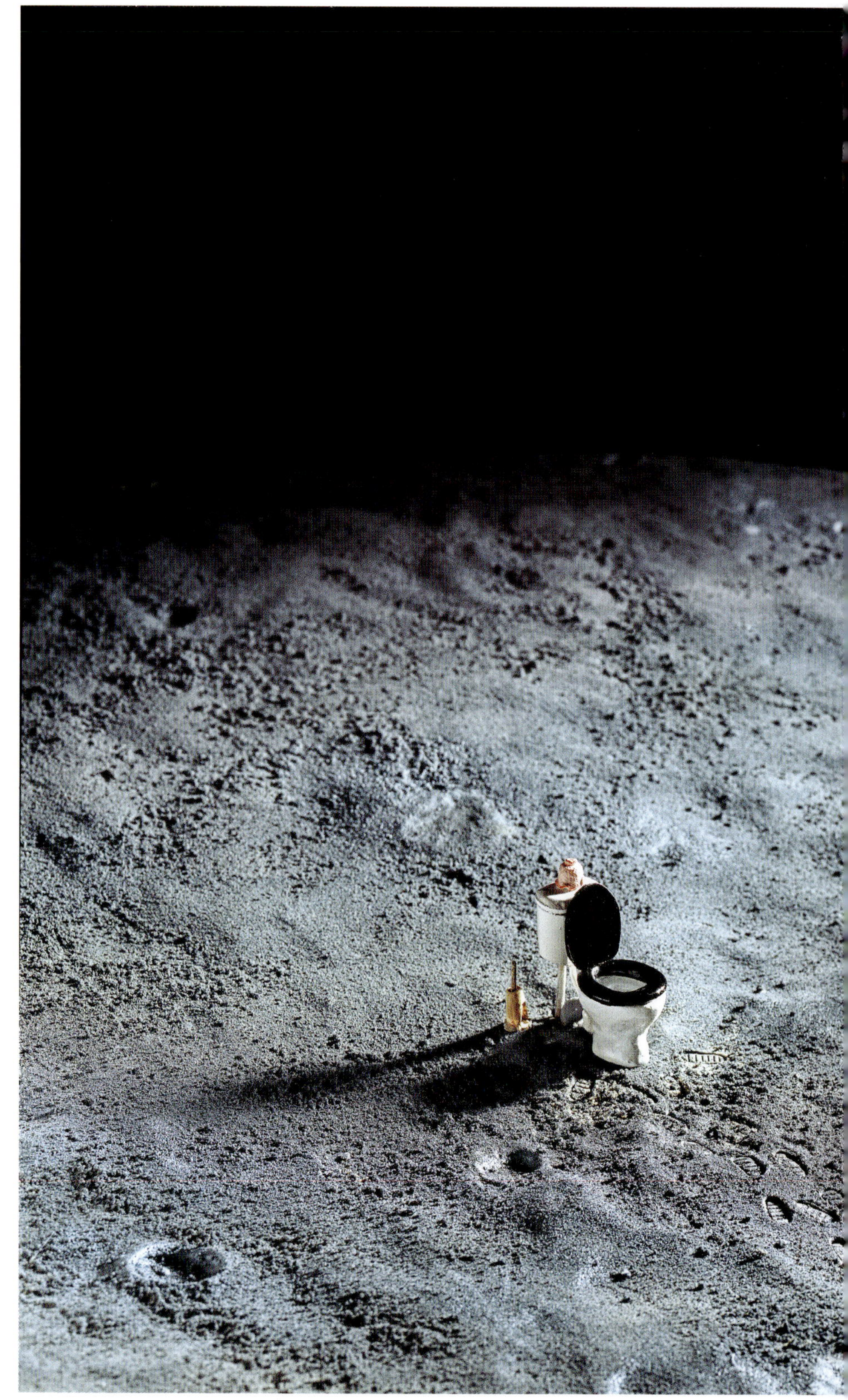

Außentoilette | Outside Toilet
2009

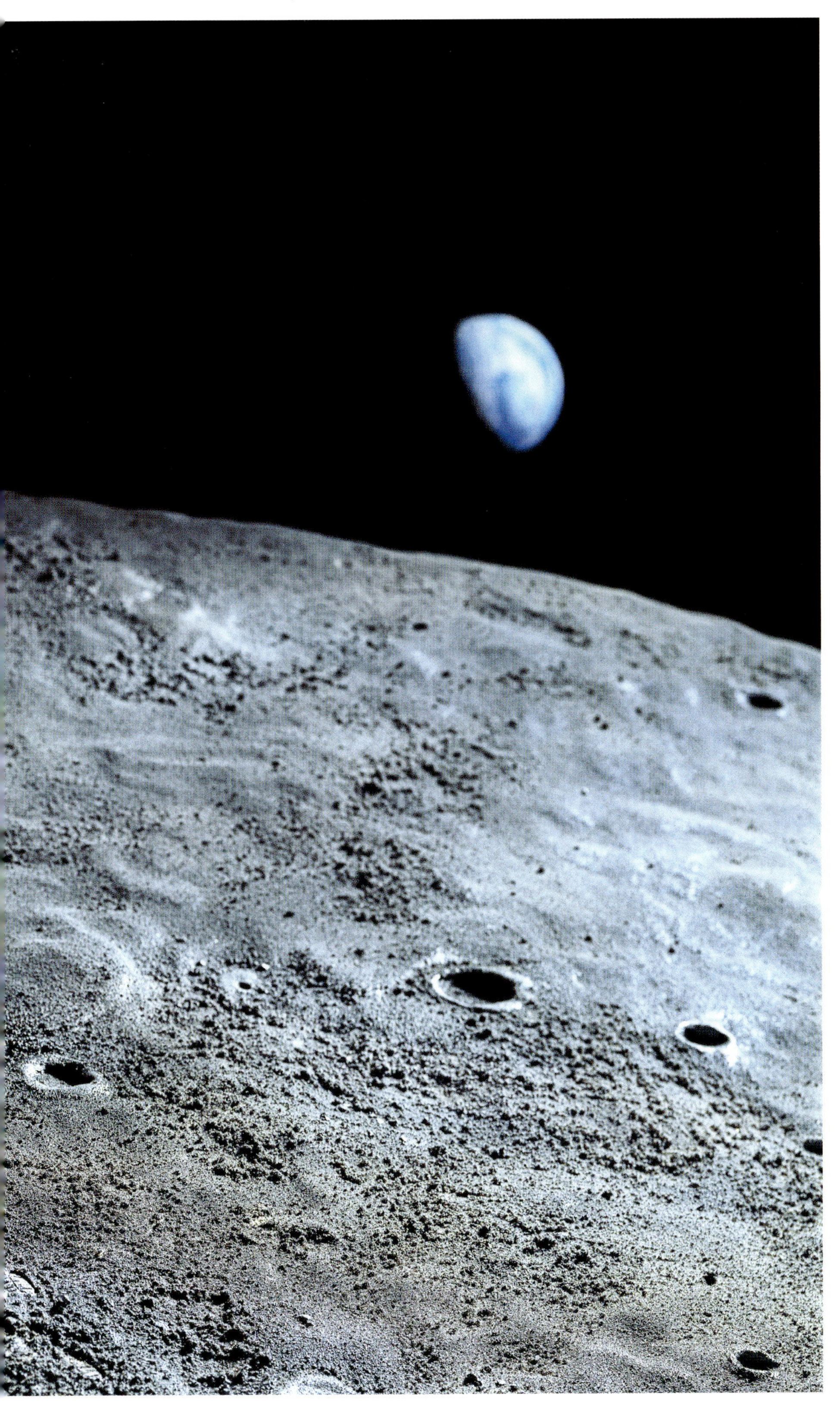

Herausgeber | Editor:
Frank Kunert

Mit einem Text von | With a text by:
Ariadne von Schirach

Projektmanagement | Project management:
Juliane Eisele, Hatje Cantz

Lektorat | Copyediting:
Pia Oddo, Dawn Michelle d'Atri

Grafische Gestaltung | Graphic design:
Rutger Fuchs Amsterdam

Reproduktion | Reproductions:
Repromayer GmbH

Verlagsherstellung | Production:
Kati Klaeske

Papier | Paper:
G-Print Smooth

Druck und Bindung | Printing and binding:
GRASPO CZ

Erschienen im | Published by
Hatje Cantz Verlag GmbH
Mommsenstraße 27
10629 Berlin
Deutschland | Germany
contact@hatjecantz.de
www.hatjecantz.com
Ein Unternehmen der Ganske Verlagsgruppe
A Ganske Publishing Group Company

ISBN: 978-3-7757-5927-4

Printed in Czech Republic

Umschlagabbildung | Front cover illustration:
Kletterurlaub | Climbing Holidays, 2017

Frontispiz | Frontispiece:
Skizze Kletterurlaub | Sketch Climbing Holidays, 2017

Seite | Page 4:
Making of Kletterurlaub | Climbing Holidays, 2017

Seite | Page 7:
Making of Life-Übertragung | Live Broadcast, 2012